Michael and Eric Scratch

PYTHON ALGORITHMS

A Complete Guide to Learn Python for Data Analysis, Machine Learning, and Coding from Scratch

Table of Contents

PREFACE 6

What Are Algorithms 7
Sample Algorithm 8
What Makes a Good Algorithm 10
Algorithm Writing Assignments 11

CHAPTER 1. OVERVIEW 16

Python Conventions 16
How Data is Structured 17
Machine Learning 19
Model Validation 20

CHAPTER 2. PERFORMANCE METRICS 24

Validation Metrics 24
Testing 29
Where to Get Our Data 37
Getting High-Quality Data 41
Have Enough Data 44

CHAPTER 3. TECHNICAL INDICATORS 46

Algorithms 46
Complexity Analysis 47
Sort Algorithms 53
Insertion Sort - time complexity O(n^2) 55
Searching Algorithms 55
Recursion 56
Model Validation 57
Robust Data Model 57
How Featurization Is Achieved 58
Important Considerations 59

CHAPTER 4. SIMULATIONS AND OPTIMIZATION 60

How to Lay the Groundwork 60
Exploring Data 62
Picking Out the Algorithms to Use 74
The Fundamental Components of the Team Data Science Process 80
Deliverables to Be Created in This Stage 85

Data Acquisition and Understanding 86
Deliverables to Be Created in This Stage 88
Modeling 88
Deliverables to Be Created in This Stage 90
Deployment 91
Deliverables to Be Created in This Stage 91
Customer Acceptance 92
Deliverables to Be Created in This Stage 93
Types of Data 93
Data Science Strategies 95
Data Science Versus Data Analysis 97
Data Science in Cyber Security 98
A Practical Example of Working with Python Data Science 99
What the Cloud Is 101

CHAPTER 5. ALTERNATIVE DATA 108

Data Exploration 108
Creating New Features 110
Dimensionality Reduction 113
Covariance Matrix 113
Gathering Your Data 115

CONCLUSION 122

Preface

There may be many different options out there that you can choose from when it comes to coding your programs, but none of them can offer you the versatility, and all of the benefits, that you are going to be able to get with Python, and that is exactly what we are going to discuss when we are in this guidebook.

To start this guidebook, we are going to take a look at a few different topics that are ever more increasingly being discussed in relation to Python.

Python is among the top programming languages that universities and industries are preferring to teach and use, respectively.

The charm of Python is hidden in the fact that it has extremely large applications in a wide range of fields.

Python is very easy to read and learn. You can easily read source codes for different programs that are created by other programmers. In the beginning, you can take the code and just paste it in the editor to see the results. In the second phase, you can make minor edits to the code and see the results. In the third phase, you will be able to completely reshape a program and see how it runs in the Python shell.

With the help of the information in this guidebook, you will be able to really work on all of this, even as a beginner, with the help of Python.

When you are ready to learn how to do some Python programming, how it can work with machine learning, deep learning, and artificial intelligence, make sure to check out this guidebook to help you get started!

What Are Algorithms

In simple terms, an algorithm refers to instructions that are arranged step by step and covering every important detail. The goal behind an algorithm is that by the time you finish following the final instruction, you would have solved a problem. The instructions in an algorithm should be arranged in a way that makes sense. That means they should be logical. You can't skip a step in the instructions. On top of that, you should also follow one step after the other in the designated order.

You can't go to step 5 then go back to step 3. One step is a prerequisite to the other steps. For instance, you can't tell someone to take a bite on sardines before you take them out of the can or maybe chop the potatoes first and then take them out of the fridge.

The right way to arrange these instructions is first to open the can of sardines first before you can eat them and take the potatoes out of the fridge, and then you can chop them up.

Think of an Algorithm as a Kind of Recipe

You need to follow the recipe exactly as it says, or else you don't get the results that you want. The same is true when you write a gaming program (or any other app or program for that matter).

You need to follow everything step by step. If you don't, you end up getting an error message, or you won't get the results that you were expecting to get. It may not be as detailed as it should be since you were supposed to fill in the rest of the tasks as part of the exercise, but those instructions are also another example of an algorithm.

Sample Algorithm

Making an algorithm can be easy with a little exercise. You can even think of algorithms for the things you do every day. In this section, we'll go over an algorithm for a simple everyday task—brushing your teeth. We'll go over the details of that task and the steps needed to accomplish it. After that, you will have to work on an assignment to outline the step by step tasks needed in another algorithm.

Brush Your Teeth Algorithm

Here is a simple algorithm for brushing your teeth.

1. Grab a tube of toothpaste in one hand and open the cap using your other hand.

2. With your other hand, grab hold of a toothbrush in an upright position with the bristles facing you.

3. Bring the tube of toothpaste that you were holding in your other hand closer to the bristles of the toothbrush.

4. Squeeze enough toothpaste onto the brush placing it on the bristles of the brush.

5. Put the tube of toothpaste down on the counter so you can begin brushing.

6. Open your mouth and smile.

7. Press the bristles of your brush against your front teeth—this will apply toothpaste on your teeth.

8. Brush your front teeth with an up and down motion.

9. Do this for 10 seconds.

10. Press your brush against the molars on your jaw near your left cheek. Brush those teeth with an in-and-out motion (aka a forward and back motion).

11. Brush for 10 seconds.

12. Press your brush against the molars on your jaw near the right cheek this time. Brush with an in and out motion.

13. Brush for 10 seconds.

14. Take the brush out of your mouth and rinse it with water from the tap.

15. Grab a glass of water and gargle. Spit the water out into the sink.

16. You are done brushing.

As you can see from this sample algorithm, the instructions are very detailed. There are also smaller tasks or sub-tasks involved in the process of brushing one's teeth, such as how to open a tube of toothpaste, how to brush the front teeth, and how to brush the inside of your mouth. There is also a sub-section for rinsing your mouth. I can bet that you can think of other sub-tasks that you can add details to in the algorithm above. Maybe you would want to add details on how to gargle or maybe how to get the toothbrush's cap/container off.

Another interesting detail that you might have also noticed is that there are tasks or steps that are repeated. An example of this is brushing the insides of the mouth. You repeat the same steps to brush the teeth near the left cheek and also for the teeth near the right cheek.

Sub-tasks, repetition of steps, and detailed and orderly procedures are all programming concepts that you can use when creating games. You start by learning how to think logically and craft an algorithm before you write your game code.

What Makes a Good Algorithm

In Python programming, there are certain qualities that will make an algorithm really good for solving a particular problem. They will be essential when you start writing game programs.

Remember the following:

- Each step in the algorithm that you will write should be unambiguous—that means whatever it is that you want to get done should be very clear.
- The input that is needed from the user and the output that should be displayed on the screen should be precisely defined.
- Do not add any computer code to the algorithm so that you can apply or make use of other programming languages to write the code based on the algorithm.

Algorithm Writing Assignments

Write 2 Parallel Lines

So, here it is. Write an algorithm that will instruct a person to write two parallel lines.

The tools that the person will use include the following:

- A pencil
- A ruler
- A sheet of Paper

Remember the techniques and details we talked about earlier. You can use repetition, sub-tasks, and orderly detailed procedures in the instructions. Use as many instructions as necessary to complete the algorithm.

Spell Hello

Here is your second assignment.

You will write an algorithm that will detail the steps to display the word Hello horizontally and then vertically.

After that, you will use the Python coding information that you have learned from the previous chapter, which is about using the print statement.

Remember that you will not only write an algorithm, but you will also write an actual Python program that will print the letters of the word "Hello" in one line and then display each of these letters in each line.

In effect, the output should look something like this:

```
H e l l o
H
e
l
l
o
```

The answer to each assignment will be on the next page.

Answer to Assignment 1

The following is an algorithm to solve the problem in assignment 1. Note that there can be different ways to solve the problem (i.e. to get the task of writing two parallel lines done).

The solution/algorithm presented below may be a bit different from the one that you may have written. It's the same thing in mathematics or in programming. There are different ways to get to a certain solution.

1. Get a piece of paper, a ruler, and a pencil.

2. Place the piece of paper on a table in portrait orientation. That means the paper should be vertically oriented, which is typical of letters, book texts, and memos. In other words, it should appear taller, not wider.

3. Place the ruler horizontally at the middle of the paper where it bisects the sheet into two equal halves.

4. Hold the rule down with one hand making sure that it doesn't move.

5. Use the pencil to draw a line on the paper by tracing it along the top edge of the ruler.

6. Make another line but this time tracing along the bottom edge of the ruler.

7. Remove the ruler from off the paper. Now you are done.

Remember that your algorithm may be a bit different than what is provided above.

Answer to Assignment 2

Here is the answer to assignment number 2. Note again that your actual solution or algorithm may be a bit different.

1. Launch the IDLE program editor.

2. Click File > New File

3. Type the following code in the "Untitled" file window that will pop up:

   print("Hello World!")

   print("H")

   print("e")

   print("l")

```
print("l")

print("o")
```

4. In that same window where you typed that Python code go to File > Save As

5. Type "Print Hello World Horizontally and Vertically" and then click "Save" at the bottom of the window.

6. Click Run > Run Module

7. You will see the output in the Python shell window.

Chapter 1.

Overview

Python Conventions

Programming Naming Conventions

Readability and consistency are vital when working on a project, especially if others have to read your work. For this reason, you need to learn about programming naming conventions. A programmer or a data analyst should be able to look through your code and understand it at a glance. It should be self-explanatory with intuitive variables that make it clear to the reader what their purpose is.

Do not ignore this aspect of programming. Someday you might write a program, hit a stump, abandon it for a short while, and when you come back to it, it will look like gibberish due to variables that have no meaning to you.

With that being said, here are the most commonly used naming conventions used by programmers and data scientists:

Pascal Case

Capitalize the first letter of each word without using any spaces or symbols between them. A variable name written using Pascal Case should look something like this: PascalCaseVariable, MyComplexPassword, CarManufacturer.

Camel Case

This is almost the same as Pascal case, except the first word starts with a lowercase letter. A variable name written using Camel Case should look something like this: camelCaseVariable, myInterface, userPassword.

Snake Case

This naming convention is often used to clearly illustrate multi-word variables by separating each word with an underscore sign. Snake Case can be applied together with Camel Case or Pascal Case.

The only thing that differentiates it from others is word separation. A variable name written using Snake Case should look something like this: my_snake_case_variable, This_is also_snake_case, my_account_password. Reading variable names might seem easier on the eye by using this naming convention. As a side note, Snake Case is also great for naming your project folders and files, and it is often used for that purpose.

Keep in mind that there is no such thing as the "best" naming convention. It all depends on your preference; however, you should always be consistent when writing your code. Try not to mix different naming conventions. Pick one style and stick to it throughout your project. Give your variables a descriptive name that allows the reader to understand what it does and then write them by using one of the mentioned conventions.

How Data is Structured

There are many different forms of data, but, at its highest level, data is mainly categorized in three ways:

Structured

This is the incredibly organized data found in databases, CSV files (as values separated by commas), or other repositories. The data format ensures it is right for computation and inquiries, using SQL or other structured languages.

Semi-Structured

Data that doesn't follow the way data models are structured when associated with data tables like relational databases but does have markers and tags that keep the semantic elements apart and enforce hierarchy in the data fields and records.

Unstructured

All the data that has no real structure, such as natural language text or audio streams.

Clearly, the most useful data is structured data because it is ready for immediate manipulation.

As a rule, only around 20% of the total data is represented by structured data, while the remaining 80% is a combination of unstructured and semi-structured data.

Be aware, though; most of what we call unstructured data does have some kind of structure. Take an article for publishing on the internet, for example.

While it is classed as unstructured, it does have a structure of sorts by way of tags and metadata for the article content. It is classed as unstructured because the content itself has no real structure that is usable straightaway.

Machine Learning

In the machine learning phase, a learning model is created and then validated. On occasion, the model itself is the product, and this would be deployed in an application context, providing some type of capability, such as prediction or classification. Other times, the algorithm is nothing more than a means to an end, and, in cases like this, the learning algorithm is not the product; the data produced by the model is.

The real meat of the pipeline lies in data processing. In one learning model, the data is processed by the algorithm, and the result is a brand-new data product. However, from the sense of production, the model is actually the product, and it is deployed as a way of adding value or providing insight, i.e., a neural network deployed for prediction for the insurance market.

There are multiple approaches to machine learning, and later we'll be looking at some of the more popular algorithms to illustrate just how rich the capabilities provided by machine learning are.

There are three primary types of machine learning:

Supervised Learning

The training data is labeled, and the dataset contains an independent variable or class; the algorithm trains to predict the right class and changes the model when it cannot make the right prediction. This continues until a certain level of accuracy is reached, and the model can then be deployed to make predictions on unseen data.

Unsupervised Learning

There is no class; the algorithm looks at the data and puts it into groups, based on a hidden structure in the data.

Reinforcement Learning

This is a type of semi-supervised algorithm that learns on a reward basis—when it makes satisfactory predictions, it is rewarded; when it doesn't, it is penalized.

Model Validation

Once a machine learning model has been trained, we want to know how it is going to behave when it goes into production. Model validation is one method used to understand this behavior. One of the commonest approaches to model validation is reserving a certain percentage of the dataset for use as test data against the finished model. The training data, typically 80% of the available data, is used for training the model. In contrast, the test data, typically 20%, is used to test the final model to see how well it can generalize when fed with unseen data.

Constructing a test data set from the training data may be complicated. You can use random sampling, but this can cause a problem. The random sample may, for example, over-sample for a specific class, or it may not provide decent coverage of all the potential data features or classes. When you do random sampling using a data class distribution, you can prevent overfitting (the training is too close to the training date) or underfitting (the training data isn't modeled, and the model cannot generalize).

Operations

This refers to the pipeline's end goal, and it can be nothing more than creating data product visualizations to tell your audience a story, or it could be to answer a specific question set before the model was trained on the dataset. It could even be as complex as the deployment of the model in production to carry out an operation on unseen data for the purpose of classification or prediction. We'll look at both now.

Model Deployment

When the machine learning product is a model that can be used against data in the future, the model is being deployed for application against new data in a production environment. That model may be a prediction system taking historical financial data as input, such as revenue and monthly sales figures, classifying whether the company is a good target for acquisition.

In a scenario such as this, the model that gets deployed is not learning any longer; it is given data from which it makes its predictions. There are some excellent reasons why learning should be avoided in production. In a deep learning context, i.e., neural networks that have deep layers, there have been some adverse attacks that can change a network's results. In a deep learning network for image processing, for example, applying a perturbation to an image can change that image's prediction capabilities in such a way that, rather than seeing a tank, the network sees a lorry. These types of adverse attacks have gotten more prevalent since deep learning became more used, and active research contains new attack vectors.

Model Visualization

Where data science is smaller in scale, the data is the product we are after, not the model the machine learning phase produces. This is one of the more common operational forms in the pipeline; the model gives us the means to provide a product (data) that can answer one or more questions about the initial dataset. There are many options in terms of data visualization, and we will learn more about that shortly when we look at how to use Matplotlib for data visualization.

Chapter 2.

Performance Metrics

Validation Metrics

In order to determine how close you are to your original objective; you have to use a scoring function. These are used to evaluate the performance of your data system by dealing with binary classification, regression, or multi-label classification. Let's discuss and examine some of the functions to understand how to use them in machine learning.

Multi-Label Classifications

A multi-label classification problem is when we need to accurately predict more than one label. How's the weather? What kind of career path are you going to take? What type of bird is this? This is an example of such a problem. Multi-label classification is often encountered, and therefore there are many ways of classifying them. Let's go through a basic example in order to gain a better understanding of this concept:

```
In: from sklearn import datasets

iris = datasets.load_iris()

from sklearn.cross_validation import train_test_split

X_train, X_test, Y_train, Y_test = train_test_split(iris.data,
```

```
iris.target, test_size=0.50, random_state=4)

from sklearn.tree import DecisionTreeClassifier

classifier = DecisionTreeClassifier(max_depth=2)

classifier.fit(X_train, Y_train)

Y_pred = classifier.predict(X_test)

iris.target_names

Out: array(['setosa', 'versicolor', 'virginica'],

dtype='<U10')
```

Now that we have the example, let’s look at which kinds of measures we can take for this type of classification.

The first thing we can do is to identify the misclassification of every class. This is done with the help of a *confusion matrix*, which is a table we can use for the previously mentioned step. Assuming that the classification is perfect, the cells of the matrix that are not set on a diagonal would contain 0 values. Let’s examine this through the example:

```
In: from sklearn import metrics

from sklearn.metrics import confusion_matrix

cm = confusion_matrix(Y_test, Y_pred)

print (cm)

Out: [[30 0 0]

[ 0 19 3]
```

```
[ 0 2 21]]

In: import matplotlib.pyplot as plt

img = plt.matshow(cm, cmap=plt.cm.autumn)

plt.colorbar(img, fraction=0.045)

for x in range(cm.shape[0]):

for y in range(cm.shape[1]):

plt.text(x, y, "%0.2f" % cm[x,y],

size=12, color='black', ha="center", va="center")

plt.show()

Out:
```

With the help of tabular visualization, we can see that in our example the first class “setosa” (class 0) is not misclassified. However, “versicolor” which is class 1 is misclassified as the “virginica” class twice. Class “virginica” (class 2) is also misclassified as versicolor twice.

Another measure we can take to identify misclassification is through the *accuracy* measure. Accuracy simply portrays how accurate the classification of labels is. Here’s an example in code:

```
In: print ("Accuracy:", metrics.accuracy_score(Y_test, Y_pred))

Accuracy: 0.933333333333
```

Another popular measure is the *precision* measure. We count the number of results that are relevant, and therefore the number of correct labels. Afterwards, a calculation is made that determines the average of all labels. Here's how it looks in code:

In: print ("Precision:", metrics.precision_score(Y_test,

Y_pred))

Precision: 0.933333333333

A third measure example is the *recall* concept. It determines how many relevant results we have and compares them to the relevant labels. Basically, the number of correct label classification is divided by the number of labels. The results of this calculation are then averaged like so:

In: print ("Recall:", metrics.recall_score(Y_test, Y_pred))

Recall: 0.933333333333

The last measure worth taking note of is the *F1 score*. This concept, however, is mostly used when we have an unbalanced dataset. The purpose of it is to determine whether our classifier is performing properly in relation to our classes. The F1 score is, in fact, the harmonic mean of recall and precision. To clarify in case you don't know, a harmonic mean is an average of rates. We're not going to dig deeper into the mathematics side of this calculation. It is enough that you gain an idea of the concept of an F1 score. Here's how it's used in code:

In: print ("F1 score:", metrics.f1_score(Y_test, Y_pred))

F1 score: 0.933267359393

There are other methods you can use in multi-label classifications; however, these are the ones you will deal with most frequently. The other step you should take after using these measures is creating a classification report. Here's how to create this report and see the results:

In: from sklearn.metrics import classification_report

print (classification_report(Y_test, Y_pred,

target_names=iris.target_names))

Out:

Now let's talk a bit more about the use of these different measures of multi-label classification. It's worth taking note that "precision" and "recall" are the ones that are used in most scenarios, especially when compared to "accuracy". Why? Simply because in the real world, the majority of data sets are not balanced. This lack of balance needs to be accounted for in data science, and this is done with precision, recall, as well as the F1 score. Also keep in mind that if you get perfect classification results, there might be an error somewhere. In the real world, there are rarely perfect solutions to problems with datasets. The "it's too good to be true" mantra truly applies when it comes to multi-label classifications especially.

Binary Classifications

Let's assume we have only two output classes. For example, when you need to guess the gender. You can use the previously mentioned methods for binary classification as well; however, you will have to take an additional step. This step is a graphical representation of the performances of a classifier, and is called the "receiver operating characteristics curve." It's also sometimes known as the "area under a curve." This graphical expression is highly informative because it displays how a change in the outcome occurs when a parameter is changed. First, it expresses the performances of the true positive rate and then the false positive rate. The true positive rate (or hit rate) represents the correct positive results, while the false positive rate (or miss rate) represents the rate of incorrect positive results. If you search for an example of a receiver operating characteristic, you will notice there's an area under the curve which expresses how the classifier performs next to a random classifier. Normally in this kind of graphical representation, the random classifier is represented through a dotted line, while the better classifier is through a solid line.

You can use the following function to build a receiver operating characteristic graph through Python:

sklearn.metrics.roc_auc_score().

Testing

So far we've loaded the data, preprocessed it, created a few new features, looked for any outliers and inaccurate data points, looked at various validation metrics, and now we are finally prepared to apply the machine learning algorithm. Machine learning algorithms observe our examples, group them with their results, and extract the rules that can be generalized to future examples by guessing their correct results.

For instance, supervised machine learning applies several learning algorithms that can predict future data. The question is, how can we apply the learning process so that we accurately predict the outcome from similar data?

To explain this part, let's import a dataset so we can directly work through an example.

In: from sklearn.datasets import load_numbers

numbers = load_ numbers()

print (numbers.DESCR)

X = numbers.data

y = numbers.target

With this "numbers" dataset, we are creating a scenario where we have a collection of images that contain handwritten numbers from 0 to 9.

Our format consists of a matrix with 8x8 images of these numbers that are stored as a vector. Flattening each 8x8 image results in this vector that will have 64 numeric values from 0 to 16.

Basically, this expresses the greyscale tonality of every single pixel contained in the images, like so:

In: X[0]

Out: array([0., 0., 5., 13., 9., 1., 0., 0., ...])

Next, we will upload three machine learning algorithms that already have their parameters set to learn. These algorithms are also known as machine learning hypotheses. Here's an example of this process:

In: from sklearn import svm

h1 = svm.LinearSVC(C=1.0)

```
h2 = svm.SVC(kernel='rbf', degree=3, gamma=0.001, C=1.0)

h3 = svm.SVC(kernel='poly', degree=3, C=1.0)
```

We are importing a linear SVC, followed by a radial basis SVC and a 3rd-degree polynomial SVC. SVC stands for support vector classification, and you can read the documentation on Scikit-learn's website:

https://scikit-learn.org/stable/modules/generated/sklearn.svm.SVC.html

Keep in mind that the purpose of this book is to introduce you to the world of data science and to teach you how to start working with Python. As an aspiring data scientist, it becomes part of your task to conduct the needed research. As the book progresses, you will have to slowly adjust to doing more and more research. We're going to discuss concepts, methodologies, and examples that illustrate them; however, as a student, you must expand on this data on your own.

With that being said, let's start by fitting the linear classifier into our data and verify the outcome:

```
In: h1.fit(X,y)

print (h1.score(X,y))

Out: 0.984974958264
```

The first learning algorithm uses an array "x" in order to predict one of ten classes that the y vector indicates. Then the "score" method analyses the performance of the specified "x" array as an average accuracy based on the true values given by the "y" vector. As you can see in the example, the prediction accuracy is roughly 98%.

This result is actually a representation of how well the learning algorithm performs. In certain cases, we will not have fresh data available. In such a scenario, the data will have to be divided into a training set and a test set. The training set will contain around 70% of the data, while the test set will contain the rest. The split should be random; however, unbalanced class distribution needs to be accounted for. Let's execute the following code; see this in practice:

```
In: chosen _state = 1

X_train, X_test, y_train, y_test = validation.train_test (X, y,

test_size=0.30, random_state=chosen_ state)

print ("(X train shape %s, X test shape %s, \ny train shape %s, y test

shape %s" \

% (X_train.shape, X_test.shape, y_train.shape, y_test.shape))

h1.fit(X_train,y_train)

print (h1.score(X_test,y_test))

# This will return the average accuracy on the test data

Out:

(X train shape (1257, 64), X test shape (540, 64),

y train shape (1257,), y test shape (540,)

0.953703703704
```

Let's discuss the block of code to see what happens. In this example, we split the total data randomly into two sets, as previously discussed. This is done with the "validation.train_test" function based on the "test_size" parameter. As a side note, this parameter can be an integer that is used to express how many examples we have for the test set, or it can be a float that indicates the percentage of data that should be utilized for testing. Afterward, the data split is ruled by "random_state" which guarantees that the process can be reproduced at any time and on any computer. This addition will also ensure that we can run and reproduce the operation on any computer, no matter which operating system is running. In our example, we have an accuracy of 0.94. If we change the value of our "chosen_ state" parameter, we will see a change in the accuracy. What does that mean? The performance evaluation is not an absolute measure, and we should use it carefully. Different test samples will yield different results. The performance result should look great as long as we're evaluating on a select test set; however, if we use a different test set, the same performance will not be replicated. The conclusion to this is that we need to decide between several hypotheses. This is a common procedure in data science. We fit each hypothesis on the training data and use a sample to compare the performance. This is when we use a validation set. For this procedure, it is recommended that the total data is split 60% for training, 20% for testing, and 20% for validation. Here's how we can adapt our previous example to consider this three-way data split and test the three algorithms we have:

In: chosen_ state = 1

X_train, X_validation_test, y_train, y_validation_test =

```
validation.train_test (X, y, test_size=.40,
random_state=chosen_ state)
X_validation, X_test, y_validation, y_test =
validation.train_test (X_validation_test,
y_validation_test, test_size=.50, random_state=chosen_
state)
print ("X train shape, %s, X validation shape %s, X test
shape %s,
\ny train shape %s, y validation shape %s, y test
shape %s\n" % \
(X_train.shape, X_validation.shape, X_test.shape,
y_train.shape,
y_validation.shape, y_test.shape))
for hypothesis in [h1, h2, h3]:
hypothesis.fit(X_train,y_train)
print ("%s -> validation mean accuracy = %0.3f" %
(hypothesis,
hypothesis.score(X_validation,y_validation)))
h2.fit(X_train,y_train)
print ("\n%s -> test mean accuracy = %0.3f" % (h2,
h2.score(X_test,y_test)))
```

Out:

X train shape, (1078, 64), X validation shape (359, 64),

X test shape (360, 64),

y train shape (1078,), y validation shape (359,),

y test shape (360,)

LinearSVC(C=1.0, class_weight=None, dual=True, fit_intercept=True,

intercept_scaling=1, loss='squared_hinge', max_iter=1000,

multi_class='ovr', penalty='l2', random_state=None, tol=0.0001,

verbose=0) -> validation mean accuracy = 0.958

SVC(C=1.0, cache_size=200, class_weight=None, coef0=0.0,

decision_function_shape=None, degree=3, gamma=0.001, kernel='rbf',

max_iter=-1, probability=False, random_state=None, shrinking=True,

tol=0.001, verbose=False) -> validation mean accuracy = 0.992

SVC(C=1.0, cache_size=200, class_weight=None, coef0=0.0,

decision_function_shape=None, degree=3, gamma='auto',

kernel='poly', max_iter=-1, probability=False, random_state=None, shrinking=True, tol=0.001, verbose=False) -> validation mean accuracy =

0.989

SVC(C=1.0, cache_size=200, class_weight=None, coef0=0.0,

decision_function_shape=None, degree=3, gamma=0.001, kernel='rbf',

max_iter=-1, probability=False, random_state=None, shrinking=True,

`tol=0.001, verbose=False) -> test mean accuracy = 0.978

You can see in the output how we distributed the total cases in percentiles to training, test, and validation cases. First, we split the data with our "validation.train_test" function into two different segments. Next, we took the test/validation set to divide it again with the same function. Afterward, we tested every single algorithm on the validation set. You can see in the results that we have an accuracy of roughly 0.99. This tells us that the best algorithm is the SVC, which is using the RBF kernel. Next, we made a decision to use this algorithm further on the test set. This gave us an accuracy of nearly 0.98. At this point, we have to question ourselves whether we used the correct algorithm. Under these circumstances, we have two different results on the validation and test sets. What you should do next is run this code at least 40 times in order to avoid any statistical noise or errors that may interfere with the results. Keep in mind that you should change the value of "random_state" every time you run the code. This way, your results will be as accurate as they can be in such a scenario.

Where to Get Our Data

The first thing that we need to work on here is how to gather our data. We want to make sure that we are collecting from some good sources and that the data is high quality and will do the work that we want at the right time. There are a number of methods that we are able to use when it comes to gathering our data, and these will include:

The first option is going to be observed. Seeing is believing with this one. It is going to include us making some direct observations of some of the things that are going on around us.

You will find that this is going to be effective and fast, a method to help collect the data that we want with just a little bit of intrusion.

The important part here is to make sure that we have the right mechanism in place to make the observations, and we are ready. There are a few advantages to working with this method, including:

- You will not have the issue of your subjects not responding to you when you make the direct observation.
- If the observation is simple and doesn't require interpretation, this model isn't going to require a lot of training in order to get it to work the way to make it work.
- The preparation time and the requirements for the infrastructure are minimal to handle the simple observations.

There are a few disadvantages that can come with using these observations, though. For example, when the observation is more complex, it is going to require some more interpretation and could lead to some bias in the process. And the analysis that you are working with could rely heavily on experts who need to know what to observe and how to interpret the observations once you have collected the data. And in some cases, there is the possibility of missing out on the complete picture because there isn't a direct interaction with the subjects of the sample.

Another option that we are able to work with is the questionnaire. This is going to be a kind of stand-alone instrument that helps us to gather data that can be administered out to the sample of subjects. You can send this out through online methods, phones, or mail. These have long been one of the most popular out of the techniques of data collection, and this can really help us to see some good results with them as well. There are a few benefits to using this kind of process, and these are going to include:

- These can help the researcher have the chance to carefully structure and even formulate the plan of data collection that they should come with some precision.

- The respondents of these are able to take the survey at the time that is the most convenient for their needs. And they can even go at their own pace when it comes to thinking through the answers

- The reach that you are able to have with this one is, in theory, limitless. These are able to reach every place that you want in the world if the medium you are using allows for it.

There are going to be some disadvantages that come with this one as well. First, if these are done without human intervention, they can be quite passive and can miss out on some of the finer points that come with this and can leave some of the responses open to interpretation. This is why adding them with some discussions in focus groups and interviews can help. The response rates of these can be low as well because it is hard to encourage the participants to actually fill them out and send the results back.

Next on the list is going to be the interviews. Conducting these interviews is a great way to help us overcome some of the shortfalls of the previous two collection techniques of data that we went through earlier because it allows you to have a better and deeper kind of understanding of the thinking that comes with the answers of the respondents. There are a few benefits that we are going to see when it comes to working with the interview, and these will include:

- These interviews are going to help the researchers to uncover deep and rich insights and learn information that could have been missed out on in other cases.

- The presence of this interviewer is going to give the respondents some additional comfort when they are done answering the questions and can ensure that you are getting the interpretation of the questions in the right way.

- The physical presence of a persistent, well-trained interviewer can significantly improve the rate of response that you are able to get.

Of course, along with some of the other options, there are going to be a few disadvantages that come with this kind of option as well. The first issue is that reaching out to all respondents to help conduct the interviews is going to be a massive and time-consuming exercise that is going to lead to a major increase in the cost of conducting the survey. And to ensure that you are making the whole exercise as effective as possible, the interviewers must be trained well in necessary soft skills and the relevant subject matter.

And the final method that we are going to take a look at is the focus group discussions. These are going to take some of the interactive benefits of an interview to the next level because you are going to bring together a carefully chosen group together for a moderated discussion on the subject of the survey that they are working with. The benefits that come with this will include:

The presence of several relevant people together at the same time will be able to encourage them to engage in a healthy form of discussion and can help researchers to uncover some new information that they may not have seen in other methods.

These can also help researchers to corroborate the facts instantly, and any of the responses that are inaccurate will most likely be countered by other members who are in the focus group as well.

This method is going to give researchers a chance to view both parts of the situation and can build up a balanced perspective when it comes to the matter at hand.

One of the disadvantages that you are able to find when it works with these focus groups is that finding the people you would like to include in this method is going to be hard. You want to find those who are relevant to the survey that you are working on, and then being able to get them to come together for a session at the same time can be a hard thing to accomplish. And if there are some members in the group who are excessively loud, it is going to subdue some of the opinions of those who are less vocal.

Another issue here is that the members who are in the focus group can often fall prey to the issue of groupthink. This means that if there is one person in the group who is really persuasive and influential, it can bury up the diversity of opinion that should come out here. The moderator of this discussion has to guard against this kind of thing happening. Other sources that we are able to use include social media, surveys that we send out to customers who have shopped with us before, and more. It is important to use as many different sources as we can, as long as they are high-quality, to ensure that we are getting the good data that is needed to form some of our analysis later on. But working with the methods that we have been talking about so far can really help to make this a reality.

Getting High-Quality Data

Another thing that we need to spend some time focusing on is the quality of the data that we are going to collect through this process. It is not going to do us much good if we end up with data that is low-quality, even if we have a ton of it to work with. The better the data that we can use, even if we end up having to take in fewer data overall, the easier it is going to be to train our algorithms and models overall.

Often the best thing that we are able to do with this is to make sure that we know what kind of data we want and how to pick out the data that will solve our particular business problem. If you just randomly go and search for and collect data, then this may provide you with a ton of data, but it is not going to provide us with the data that we need necessarily.

This means that we need to make sure that we are going with data that is going to solve our business problem. And knowing what this business problem is, and the one that is the most important for us to solve and work on first, you will find that this will help us to pick out the option that is best for your needs. When you know what business problem you would like to focus on, you will find that it is much easier to work with this process, and we can search through some of the data that we have and the right sources to answer that business question.

It is also important to make sure that you are going with sources that are going to help you to get some high-quality data as well. You don't want to waste your time on getting data that do not form the customers who don't shop with you, or from a source that is going to have a lot of bias that will mess with the results. You need data that is accurate, matches up to the topic that you are looking to work with, and more.

First, we need to make sure that we are picking out data that is accurate and going to help keep our algorithms as strong as possible. If your data is not accurate, it is going to give you some bad results out of your algorithms. You need to make sure that all of the data that you plan to use in your algorithms is as accurate as possible so that you can train the algorithm and get the insights and more that you are looking for.

Then we need to spend some time looking at the sources we are working with and that the data is not going to have a bias or other issue with it. If you are using third-party surveys and information to help you out, you need to use some critical thinking to help out with it. We need to make sure that there is not any bias in it, that we make sure that there aren't any issues with it, and that the sampling size is big enough to help us.

A good place to start is to figure out who did the report, or at least who paid for it. This can sometimes give us some good information on the data and can help us to figure out whether or not this is the data that we are able to rely on for some of our needs.

We also need to focus on making sure that the sample size is big enough and that it actually reaches the people you want. You do not want to sample people who are in the 45 to 55 group if your customers are 25 to 35 year old's. You may find some good insights into this, but the insights are not going to be what you are looking for, and you will not get the answers that you want for your demographics.

With this in mind, we also have to make sure that we are going through and picking out the right number of people in our sample. If we have 100,000 customers and we only sample 10 of them, we are not going to get a good idea of how our customers are going to feel about something. We need to figure out how large the original size of the individuals are, and then decide what percentage of those people we would like to talk to when it is time to focus on this. That will ensure that the answers that we are working with will be accurate and can actually help us through this process.

Have Enough Data

The next question that we are going to come up with here is whether or not we have enough data to work with for our project. This is kind of a tricky process, and it is often going to depend on what you are trying to figure out and how much data you are able to gather in the first place.

The more data, the better in most cases, but you also do not want to go through and gather data for years on end before you get to create some of the algorithms that you want to work with. You have to have some kind of stopping point and know where that is so that you will have enough data, and can still get the algorithm done in a good amount of time.

When you take a look at your data warehouse, and you see that you have a good amount of data at your disposal to work with, you will find that it is time to work with the algorithms that you want to use. You can then split it up into the testing and the training set that you want to work with and can send this through for your needs. You can continue to collect information at this time as well because you may have to go through and do the training and the testing phases more than once as well.

Then when you are done with the training and the testing, you may find that you need some more data in order to make it easier for us to learn about the insights and the patterns and make some of the major decisions that are needed. When we are able to make all of this come together for our needs, you will be able to see some great results in the process.

Your goal with all of this is to make sure that you are able to gather as much information as you can, but set a limit on when you would like to get the information. This will help you to stay on track and ensure that you are not going to end up with an endless process of gathering the data without ever getting to use it to make some of the major decisions that you would like.

Gathering up the data that you would like to use when it comes to working on a data science project is going to be important. When you are able to set this up in the right manner, and you are careful with some of the work that you are doing in order to help you get started, and then you are able to use this through in order to learn more from it overall.

Chapter 3.

Technical Indicators

Algorithms

An algorithm is a set of unambiguous steps which should provide the solution to a problem after feeding input to it. There are three main categories of algorithms: the greedy, the divide and conquer, and the dynamic programming algorithms, as explained below. The Greedy algorithms try to find an optimum solution locally, which leads to globally optimized solutions. They do it by searching for the best solution at present without considering the best solution in the future. Unfortunately, in many cases, greedy algorithms do not provide globally optimized solutions. Some famous greedy algorithms are:

- Travelling Salesman Problem
- Prim's Minimal Spanning Tree Algorithm
- Kruskal's Minimum Spanning Tree Algorithm
- Dijkstra's Minimum Spanning Tree Algorithm

The Divide and Conquer algorithms involve breaking down the given problem into smaller ones and then solving each of the subproblems independently. When the problem cannot be further subdivided, then the merging process starts where the different sub-solutions are put together to create a global solution. Some famous Divide and Conquer algorithms are:

- Merge Sort
- Quick Sort
- Kruskal's Minimum Spanning Tree Algorithm
- Binary Search

The Dynamic programming algorithms involve dividing the bigger problem into smaller ones but unlike divide and then solve all of them dependently. Before solving a subproblem, a dynamic algorithm will try to examine the results of the previously solved subproblems. The dynamic algorithms are trying to provide an overall optimized solution and not the best local one.

Some famous Dynamic programming algorithms are:

- Fibonacci number series
- Knapsack problem
- Tower of Hanoi

Complexity Analysis

Algorithm Analysis

We can measure the performance of an algorithm according to two factors: time and space complexity, which define the running time and the storage space accordingly, in terms of input data with size n.

Time Complexity

Here, we do not make an accurate measurement of the running time, but we just measure its order of magnitude. Operations such as single additions, multiplications, assignments, etc., are not important and have constant time complexity, which corresponds to O(1), but operations such as for and while loops are the ones that increase the space complexity. The Big-O notation is used to measure the time complexity, and O(1) is the lowest one. When we have a simple operation or more, in a for loop (or a while loop) that will be repeated n times, e.g.:

```
k = 0
for i in range(n):

print(i)

k = k + 1
```

Then we just measure this time complexity as O(n), and if we have nested loops we multiple their time complexities:

```
k = 0
for i in range(n):
for j in range(m):

print(i)
k = k + 1
```

Or

```
k = 0
for i in range(n):
while j<m:
print(i)
j = j - 1
```

In both cases, we have O(n*m). The same stands if in a loop with time complexity n we call a function(s) with time complexity m. So, when calculating the complexity, we omit constants: i.e., regardless of whether the loop is executed 10 * n times or more, we still have time complexity equal to O(n). When analyzing the complexity, we must look for specific, worst-case examples of data that the program will take a long time to process. There are the following possible time complexities:

Linear time — O(n)

```
def linear(n, A):
for i in range(n):
if A[i] == 0:
return 0

return 1
```

*Quadratic time — O(n**2)*

```
def quadratic(n):
result = 0
for i in range(n):
for j in range(i, n):

result += 1
return result
```

Linear time — O(n + m)

```
def linear2(n, m):
result += i

for j in range(m):
result += j

return result
```

Exponential and Factorial Time

It is worth knowing that there are other types of time complexity, such as factorial time O(n!) and exponential time O(2**n). Algorithms with such complexities can solve problems only for very small values of n because they would take too long to execute for large values of n.

Time Limit

When solving a problem, you can understand the desired solution's time complexity by the problem's description. Remember the following pairs of a solution – time complexity:

n <= 1 000 000, the expected time complexity is O(n) or O(n* log n),
n <= 10 000, the expected time complexity is O(n**2),
n <= 500, the expected time complexity is O(n**3).

Of course, these limits are not precise. They are just approximations and will vary depending on the specific task. Below you can see different solutions to the same problem, which correspond to different time complexities.
Exercise Problem: You are given an integer n. Count the sum 1+2+ ... + n.

Slow solution — time complexity O(n**2)

```
def slow_solution(n):
result = 0
for i in range(n):

for j in range(i + 1):

result += 1
```

return result
Fast solution — time complexity O(n) def fast_solution(n):
result += (i + 1)

return result
Model solution — time complexity O(1)

def model_solution(n):
result = n * (n + 1) // 2

return result

Space Complexity

The memory has a limit, so it is important to have a solution that does not take too much space. Often, we have to trade time for space complexity and the opposite. The space complexity depends on the number of variables that you can declare in your program. If you have a constant number of variables, then you have a constant space complexity: in Big-O notation this is O(1). If you need to declare an array with n elements, you have linear space complexity — O(n). Be careful while calculating the space complexity, the space required to store certain data and variables that are independent of the size of the problem. For example, simple variables and constants used, program size, etc. correspond to O(1) while the space required by variables, whose size depends on the size of the problem corresponds to, e.g., O(n), where n the size of the array. Below you can see different solutions to the same problem, which correspond to different space complexities.

Exercise Problem: You are given an integer n. Count the sum 1+2+ ... + n.

Slow solution — space complexity O(1) def slow_solution(n):

result = 0
for i in range(n):
for j in range(i + 1):

result += 1

return result

Fast solution — space complexity O(1) def fast_solution(n):
result = 0

for i in range(n):
result += (i + 1)
return result

Model solution — space complexity O(1)

def model_solution(n):

result = n * (n + 1) // 2

return result

Calculations With Big-O Notation

O(c) -> O(c), where c is a constant
O(c*n) -> O(n), where c is a constant and n is a variable
O(c*n + c) -> O(n), where c is a constant and n is a variable

O(n+ n**2 + n**3) -> O(n**3), where n is a variable
O(c+n**2+c*n**3) - > O(n**3), where c is a constant and n is a variable

O(k-m) -> O (k-m), where k, m are variables
O(k+m) -> O (k+m), where k, m are variables

O(k-c*m) -> O (k-c*m), where k, m are variables and c is a constant

O(c*k+m) -> O (c*k+m), where k, m are variables and c is a constant

Sort Algorithms

The following sorting algorithms are described as they are given here: https://www.tutorialspoint.com/python_data_structure/python_sorting_algorithms.htm

There are different algorithms that sort a list in ascending or descending order. We can order the elements of a list in numerical or lexicographical order according to their type. We choose to sort a list to facilitate data searching and make our list more readable. Below you can see three sort algorithms that, given a list, return it in ascending order, and they trade time and space complexity.

- Bubble Sort
- Merge Sort
- Insertion Sort

Bubble Sort - time complexity O(n^2)

```
defbubblesortlist):
# Swap the elements to arrange in order

foriter_num inrange(len(list)-1,0,-1):

foridx inrange(iter_num):

iflist[idx]>list[idx+1]:
```

temp =list[idx
list[idx]=list[idx+1

list[idx+1]=temp

Merge Sort - time complexity O(n(logn)) **def**merge_sort
unsorted_list**):**
iflen**(**unsorted_list**)<=**1

return*unsorted_list*
Find the middle point and divide it

middle =lenunsorted_list**)**// 2

left_list =unsorted_list**[:**middle

right_list =unsorted_list**[**middle**:]**

left_list =merge_sort**(**left_list

right_list =merge_sort**(**right_list

returnlist**(**merge**(**left_list,right_list**))**

Merge the sorted halves
defmergeleft_halfright_half**):**
res =**[]**
whilelen**(**left_half**)!=**0**and**len**(**right_half**)**
!=0

ifleft_half**[**0**]**<right_half**[**0**]:**
res**.**append**(**left_half**[**0**])**
left_half**.remove(**left_half**[**0**])**

```
else
res.append(right_half[0])
right_half.remove(right_half[0])

iflen(left_half)==0
res =res +right_half
else
res =res +left_half
returnres
```

Insertion Sort - time complexity O(n^2)

```
definsertion_sortInputList):

fori inrange1,len(InputList)):
j =i-
nxt_element =InputListi

# Compare the current element with next one
whileInputList[j]>nxt_element)and( j >=0):

InputList[j+1]=InputList[j
j=-

InputList[+1]=nxt_element
```

ote: The built-in Python .sort() function has time complexity O(nlogn)

Searching Algorithms

Very often in programming, we want to search for a value in a data structure; the easiest way with the highest time complexity is to do a *linear search* (start from the beginning and search the elements of the data structure one by one until we find what we are looking for).

An alternative here is the *interpolation search*, where first we have to sort the data structure and then start searching by following the steps below:

We check if the element that we are looking for is the one in the middle of the list. If it is, we return its index, and we are done. If not:

1. If the middle item is greater than the item, then the probable position is again calculated in the subarray to the right of the middle item. Otherwise, the item is searched in the subarray to the left of the middle item. This process continues on the subarray as well until the size of the subarray reduces to zero.

2. If the search finishes and the element is not found, then the element was not included in the list.

Recursion

We say that a function works recursively when it calls itself. When it does, the same code is used for different values. This creates a clean code with low space complexity, but it can significantly increase the time complexity. It is of high importance to set criteria that will end the recursive process. Below we see the Fibonacci sequence solved recursively and iteratively, where the Fibonacci sequence starts with 0 and 1 and each next element is the sum of the previous two: 0,1,1,2,3,5,8,13. The n-th element is the sum of the n-1 and n-2 element, for n > 2 and is 0 or 1 for n = 0 or n = 1 respectively.

recursively
deffib(n):

```
ifn<=:
returnn
returnfib(n-1)+fib(n-2)

# iteratively
defFib(n):
f = (n+1)*[0]
f[]=0
f[]=1
fori inrange(,n+1):

f[i] = f[i-1]+f[i-2]
returnf[n]
```

Model Validation

Data modeling is an important aspect of Data Science. It is one of the most rewarding processes that receive the most attention among learners of Data Science. However, things aren't the same as they might look because there is so much to it rather than applying a function to a given class of package.

The biggest part of Data Science is assessing a model to make sure that it is strong and reliable. In addition, Data Science modeling is highly associated with building information feature set. It involves different processes that make sure that the data at hand is harnessed in the best way.

Robust Data Model

Robust data models are important in creating the production. First, they must have better performance depending on different metrics. Usually, a single metric can mislead the way a model performs because there are many aspects of the classification problems.

Sensitivity analysis describes another important aspect of Data Science modeling. This is something that is important for testing a model to make sure it is strong. Sensitivity refers to a condition in which the output of a model is meant to change considerably if the input changes slightly. This is very undesirable because it must be checked since the robust model is stable.

Lastly, interpretability is an essential aspect, even though it is not always possible. This is usually related to how easy one can interpret the results of a model. But most modern models resemble black boxes. This makes it hard for one to interpret them. Besides that, it is better to go for an interpretable model because you might need to defend the output from others.

How Featurization Is Achieved

For a model to work best, it must require information that has a rich set of features. The latter is developed in different ways. Whichever the case, cleaning the data is a must. This calls for fixing issues with the data points, filling missing values where it is possible, and in some situations, removing noisy elements.

Before the variables are used in a model, you must perform normalization on them. This is achieved using a linear transformation on making sure that the variable values rotate around a given range. Usually, normalization is enough for one to turn variables into features once they are cleaned.

Binning is another process that facilitates featurization. It involves building nominal variables which can further be broken down into different binary features applied in a data model.

Lastly, some reduction methods are important in building a feature set. This involves building a linear combination of features that display the same information in fewer dimensions.

Important Considerations

Besides the basic attributes of Data Science modeling, there are other important things that a Data Scientist must know to create something valuable. Things such as in-depth testing using specialized sampling, sensitivity analysis, and different aspects of the model performance to improve a given performance aspect belong to Data Science modeling.

Chapter 4.

Simulations and Optimization

How to Lay the Groundwork

Before we try to implement a brand-new technology of any sort, there are going to be a few types of steps that we need to take and go through to see the results. Not only it is important for us to have a nice solid grasp on the data that we want to use, which is something that should happen during the data analysis part of the process, but we also need to understand three other important things, including the needs of the company, the goals of the company, and the audience of your company. Some of the things that have to happen before you can prepare and organize all of the data that you have and complete this kind of data visualization will include:

Understand the data that we need to visualize in the first place. This means that we need to know how much cardinality is present in the data, meaning how much uniqueness is going to show up in the columns, and we need to know the size of the data. Some of the algorithms that we will use to work on the data visualization are not going to do as well when it comes to very large sets of data. Determine what you would like to visualize and the kind of information that we want to be able to communicate with this. This will make it a bit easier to figure out which type of visual we want to be able to go within this process.

Know the audience that we are working with and understand how they are going to process the visual information that you want to show off. Management may need a different visual than a team. Those in manufacturing may need a different visual than someone in a more creative role. Being able to make the visual fit the audience so that they can actually utilize the information is going to be a critical step.

Use a visual that is able to convey the information in a form that is not only the best but also the simplest for your audience. There are a lot of cool visuals out there that you can work with, and they can offer a lot of different ways to show your data. But if the visual is too difficult to understand, it is not going to make anyone happy. Put away some of the neat gadgets and find the best way to showcase that information that makes the most sense to your audience.

Once you have been able to go through and answer all of the initial questions that we had about the data type that we would like to work with, and you know what kind of audience is going to be there to consume the information, it is time for us to make some preparations for the amount of data that we plan to work within this process

Keep in mind here that big data is great for many businesses and is often necessary to make data science work. But it is also going to bring in a few new challenges to the visualization that we are doing. Large volumes, varying velocities, and different varieties are all going to be taken into account with this one.

Plus, data is often going to be generated at a rate that is much faster than it can be managed and analyzed, so we have to figure out the best way to deal with this problem.

There are factors that we need to consider in this process as well, including the cardinality of the columns that we want to be able to work with. We have to be aware of whether there is a high level of cardinality in the process or a low level. If we are dealing with high cardinality, this is a sign that we are going to have a lot of unique values in our data. A good example of this would include bank account numbers since each individual would have a unique account number. Then it is possible that your data is going to have a low cardinality. This means that the column of data that you are working with will come with a large percentage of repeat values. This is something that we may notice when it comes to the gender column on our system. The algorithm is going to handle the amount of cardinality, whether it is high or low, in a different manner, so we always have to take this into some consideration when we do our work.

Exploring Data

The first phase within the data science workflow is performing the exploratory analysis. You need to gain a more detailed understanding of the data you are going to work with. This implies learning about the dataset's features, the shape of the elements, and using everything in order to form your hypothesis so that you can continue with the next steps. In this section, we are going to continue working with the Iris dataset because it is very beginner-friendly, and you are already somewhat familiar with it. So start by importing the dataset once more and create a new file as you did in the previous section. Once you've performed that step, we can start exploring and go where no aspiring data scientist has gone before.

Puns aside, we are going to use the describe function first in order to learn a bit more about our dataset:

In: iris.describe()

Now you should have access to various features such as deviation, minimum and maximum values, and so on. We need to take this basic data and analyze it at a deeper level, so let's start by exploring a graphical representation of it. For now, we are going to use the simple "boxplot" function to create the plot and not bother with Matplotlib just yet.

In: boxes = iris.boxplot(return_type='axes')

Keep in mind that you don't have to perform this step. Visualization is actually optional unless you have to present your findings to someone who isn't very mathematically inclined, but he or she can understand charts and plots much easier. For the same reason, as a beginner, you should visualize your data so that you can place your focus elsewhere. Now, let's observe the relation between our features. For this step, we are going to use a similarity matrix like this:

In: pd.crosstab(iris['petal_length'] > 3.758667, iris['petal_width'] > 1.198667)

You will notice that we are simply calculating the number of times the petal length appears when compared to the petal width. We are making this comparison with the crosstab function. If you look at the results, you will see these features are well-related to each other. You can observe this even better by creating a scatterplot like so:

In: scatterplot = iris.plot(kind='scatter', x='petal_width',

```
y='petal_length', s=64, c='blue', edgecolors='white')
```

The scatterplot makes it easy to see that the petal width is connected to the length. When exploring data this way, you can also use a different kind of graph, namely a histogram. In our case, we are going to use one in order to see a display of the distribution of the values.

```
In: distr = iris.petal_width.plot(kind='hist', alpha=0.5, bins=20)
```

In this case, we have selected twenty bins. If you aren't familiar with histograms, you should know that bins refer to a variable's intervals. This is calculated by determining the square root of the total count of observations. That value represents the total number of bins.

New Features

Unfortunately, we are rarely so lucky to discover a close connection between certain features like we did in our basic example. That's when we need to apply a series of transformations. Let's say that you are trying to determine the value of a house. All you know for certain is the size of each room. You can use this information to create a new feature that represents the construction's volume. This transformation needs to be applied because we cannot observe the volume; however, we can observe features like length, width, and height and then use these features to calculate the volume. Here's how all of this can be applied with code:

```
In: import numpy as np

from sklearn import datasets
```

```
from sklearn.cross_validation import train_test_split

from sklearn.metrics import mean_squared_error

cali = datasets.california_housing.fetch_california_housing()

X = cali['data']

Y = cali['target']

X_train, X_test, Y_train, Y_test = train_test_split(X, Y, train_size=0.8)
```

(Source: California Housing dataset

https://scikitlearn.org/stable/modules/generated/sklearn.datasets.fetch_california_housing.html retrieved in October 2019)

This time we imported a new dataset called California housing, which contains a great deal of data on the Californian housing market. In this example, we are going to implement a regressor together with a mean absolute error with a value of 1.1575. If the code is difficult to understand and you don't know what a regressor is, don't worry about it at this time; we will discuss this later.

All you need to understand for now is the concept we're discussing.

```
In: from sklearn.neighbors import KNeighborsRegressor

regressor = KNeighborsRegressor()

regressor.fit(X_train, Y_train)

Y_est = regressor.predict(X_test)
```

print ("MAE=", mean_squared_error(Y_test, Y_est))

Out: MAE= 1.15752795578

Now we need to try and reduce the value of the mean absolute error by implementing Z scores. This way we can perform the regression comparison and feature normalization. This process is also known as Z normalization because it seeks to map all of the original features to the new features we created. Let's continue:

In: from sklearn.preprocessing import StandardScaler

scaler = StandardScaler()

X_train_scaled = scaler.fit_transform(X_train)

X_test_scaled = scaler.transform(X_test)

regressor = KNeighborsRegressor()

regressor.fit(X_train_scaled, Y_train)

Y_est = regressor.predict(X_test_scaled)

print ("MAE=", mean_squared_error(Y_test, Y_est))

Out: MAE= 0.432334179429

The value of the mean absolute error has now been reduced from the previous value of approximately 1.15 to nearly 0.4, which is quite a great result. There are other methods that can be employed in order to minimize this value, however, the transformations required would be too complicated to implement at this state.

What you should gain from this example is the fact that basic transformations can be easily applied and they can make your exploratory analysis much easier to conduct.

Dimensionality Reduction

In the real world, you will often work with datasets that contain tens of thousands of data items, if not hundreds of thousands. Such datasets tend to also contain a large number of features, which means there will be some of them that you will not need. Just because the information exists, that doesn't mean it's useful. In some cases, features are simply irrelevant, and they just contribute to the noise. Noise is one of the elements which reduce the accuracy of your analysis, and anything you can do to reduce it translates to an accuracy boost. When noise is caused by irrelevant features, your best option is to use dimensionality reduction methods.

As the name suggests, dimensionality reduction is all about reducing useless features and cutting back on the time that it takes to process your data. In this section, we are going to discuss a couple of techniques and algorithms you can use to eliminate the features you don't need.

Covariance Matrix

As mentioned earlier, you need to compare all of your features, or collections of features, in order to determine whether a relationship exists between them. You don't want to eliminate useful features. The covariance matrix is one of the techniques you'll be using to achieve this.

Dimensionality reduction implies the detection of relevant features, as well as the removal of the rest. Once you detect the ones that don't offer much, you can eliminate them. To demonstrate this concept, we are going to once again import the Iris dataset. Remember that this dataset contains four features for each observation; therefore, a correlation matrix will yield some useful results.

```
In: from sklearn import datasets

import numpy as np

iris = datasets.load_iris()

cov_data = np.corrcoef(iris.data.T)

print (iris.feature_names)

print (cov_data)
```

And this is how your output should look as a result.

```
['sepal length (cm)', 'sepal width (cm)', 'petal length (cm)',

'petal width (cm)']

[[ 1. -0.10936925 0.87175416 0.81795363]

[-0.10936925 1. -0.4205161 -0.35654409]

[ 0.87175416 -0.4205161 1. 0.9627571 ]

[ 0.81795363 -0.35654409 0.9627571 1. ]]
```

With the covariance matrix in place, let's create a visual representation of our results in order to have an easier time drawing conclusions. As a beginner, you should always use visualization methods because they are so much easier to read than pure numbers.

This time we are going to import Matplotlib to draw the plot for us:

```
In: import matplotlib.pyplot as plt

img = plt.matshow(cov_data, cmap=plt.cm.rainbow)

plt.colorbar(img, ticks=[-1, 0, 1], fraction=0.045)

for x in range(cov_data.shape[0]):

for y in range(cov_data.shape[1]):

plt.text(x, y, "%0.2f" % cov_data[x,y],

size=12, color='black', ha="center", va="center")

plt.show()
```

You will notice that this time we haven't used a scatterplot or a histogram. In fact, we created a heat map. Take note of the most important value, which is 1. Every feature covariance has been normalized to a value of one in order to help us see the powerful connection between a number of features.

By analyzing the heat map, you will notice that feature one has a strong relation to feature three, as well as four.

The third feature is also strongly connected to the fourth feature. Finally, we have feature two, which seems to have no relation to any of the other features. It is completely independent.

Now that you know which features are useful and which one is irrelevant, you can cut some of the useless information.

Principal Component Analysis

The next step is to use an algorithm like the principal component analysis in order to define smaller features from their parent features. The new ones will be linear, however. This means that the output's first factor will have most of the variance. The second vector will have the most of the left over variance, and so on. The information will be aggregated to a new set of vectors that are formed after employing a principal component analysis.

The implementation relies on the fact that the vectors contain the data that comes from the input, and everything else is just noise. All you need to do in this case is to decide the number of vectors to have. The decision is made based on the variance, however. Let's take a look at the practical approach to this algorithm:

```
In: from sklearn.decomposition import PCA

pca_2c = PCA(n_components=2)

X_pca_2c = pca_2c.fit_transform(iris.data)

X_pca_2c.shape

Out: (150, 2)

In: plt.scatter(X_pca_2c[:,0], X_pca_2c[:,1], c = iris.target,

alpha=0.8, s=60, marker='o', edgecolors='white')

plt.show()

pca_2c.explained_variance_ratio_.sum()
```

Out:

0.9776317750248033

(Adapted from https://educationalresearchtechniques.com/2018/10/24/factor-analysis-in-python/)

After the implementation, you will see that we only have two features in our output. The principal component analysis object is represented by the "n_components" object and its value is equal to two, which translates to what we just discussed.

We aren't going to dig deeper into the principal component analysis algorithm because it would just add an additional layer of confusion. For now, as a beginner, you should understand the concept of dimensionality reduction and not the inner workings of the algorithm. However, if you wish, you are encouraged to explore further. For now, we are going to move on to discussing another dimensionality reduction technique, namely the latent factor analysis.

Latent Factor Analysis

This concept is similar to the principal component analysis. The main idea here is that a latent factor always exists somewhere.

Take note that a latent factor is just a variable, which cannot be observed through direct methods. We can only assume that our features are affected by a latent variable. This type of variable contains a specific kind of noise known as an arbitrary waveform generator.

With that being said, let’s see how this methodology is used for dimensionality reduction.

```
In: from sklearn.decomposition import FactorAnalysis

fact_2c = FactorAnalysis(n_components=2)

X_factor = fact_2c.fit_transform(iris.data)

plt.scatter(X_factor[:,0], X_factor[:,1], c=iris.target,

alpha=0.8, s=60, marker='o', edgecolors='white')

plt.show()
```

(Adapted from: https://educationalresearchtechniques.com/2018/10/24/factor-analysis-in-python/)

The difference in this case is that we establish the covariance between the variables in the output.

Outlier Detection

This next stage is one of the most important ones. Determining outliers is important because if we have any kind of erroneous information in our dataset, or partially incomplete data, adapting any new data will be extremely problematic. In turn, this issue can lead to algorithms that proccss faulty data and create inaccurate results.

So what is an outlier in this case? When we detect that a data point deviated from other data points, we can compare them and establish that it is, in fact, an outlier. Let’s discuss several cases where we have a different outlier in order to gain a better understanding of how to detect them and treat them.

Mainly there are three situations, and each one is handled differently. Firstly, we will presume that the outlier is an infrequent appearance in whatever dataset we are working with. In this scenario, the information is based on another set of data from which it was extracted. Here we have a data sample that contains an outlier that is flagged as one because of its assumed rarity. This type of outlier is dealt with through a basic removal process. In the second example, we have an outlier that frequently manifests itself. In this case, it appears frequently. Whenever you experience similar occurrences, there's a sizable chance of encountering an error that affects the data sample generation. The problem here is that the algorithm's priority isn't the generalization; instead, it focuses on learning the non-focused distribution. The outlier has to be eliminated.

The third situation involves a data point, which is easy to conclude that it is, in fact, an error. Datasets often contain faulty data entries, and they can easily cause inconsistencies in your data whenever you modify or manipulate the value. All you need to do in this case is delete the value and instruct the model to presume that it is a random loss. Another option is calculating and using an average value instead of the erroneous one. This is a preferable solution; however, if you find it difficult to implement it, then simply delete the outlier.

Knowing these scenarios will help you understand which one you are experiencing, thus allowing you to have an easier time detecting the outlier and removing it. The first phase is to determine every single outlier and locate it. You can use two techniques to do this, though they are similar. You can either examine all separated variables individually or all of them at once. These techniques are called univariate and multivariate analysis.

Picking Out the Algorithms to Use

The first thing that we need to consider here is which of the different algorithms we are going to use. There are a number of algorithms that we are able to handle. And it is going to take some time to really ensure that we pick out the right one depending on the data that we want to work with and the types of information that we are working with when it comes to our data.

There are a lot of algorithms that we are able to handle, and they are going to fall under three main styles of machine learning, which is the idea that is going to really push and run our algorithms. These are going to include supervised learning, unsupervised learning, and reinforcement learning.

We are going to explore these in more detail in the next chapter. But we can take a moment to look through these here as well. To start with, we have supervised learning. This is where we are going to show a lot of examples to the algorithm with the right answers to the end. This helps the program to learn from these examples. Then we are able to test it on the knowledge it learns as we go through this process.

Then it is time to work with unsupervised learning. This one is a bit different because we are not going to show the algorithm the results with the example that we use. We expect the program to be able to learn all on its own. Instead, we are going to take the time to have the program learn on its own. This takes a bit more time for the program to learn and gain the right accuracy that we want. But when it gets to this point, you will find that the unsupervised learning is going to be really strong and can take on a lot more options and program capabilities than we will be able to go with all of the other choices. And then we can move on to reinforcement learning. This one is going to take us to another level as well, though, in the beginning, it is going to look like it is pretty much the same as the unsupervised learning that we were talking about above. The main difference that we are going to see with this one is that we will set this up in more of a trial and error kind of method. Reinforcement learning is going to work on trial and error and will be able to learn when it does things wrong or gets the wrong answer. It will remember all of this and work from there in order to get more accuracy. It learns on its own but has a set of rewards and punishments to help reinforce the kind of learning that we are trying to work with.

All of these can be important in helping us to handle some of the different things that we want to do with our data analysis. Since all of them are different, though, we need to make sure that we are going through and choosing the one that will help us out with our needs.

Take your time when you pick out the algorithms that you want to work with. There are tons of options, and all of them have benefits and some negatives that you need to work with as well. Learning about some of the different types and how they work is going to help us to really work through our data and find the results that we want.

Training Our Data

The next thing on the list that we need to explore is how to train our data. It would be nice to pick out the algorithm we want to run, throw the data into it, and then use the results that come out of that, knowing that they are accurate right from the beginning. But this is not the way things actually work. We need to take some time to work with that algorithm and train it to behave well.

This is where we will need to take all of that data that we found and worked through in the last chapter and split it up. We need to have at least two categories here. We will have one to be in our training set and one that will be a part of our testing set. Each of these is going to have their own roles to follow and can be important to ensure that we are going to be able to teach our algorithms the proper way to behave.

First, we have the training data set. This is the set of data that we are going to use in order to make it easier to teach the algorithm how to behave. We will show the data with the corresponding right answers along with it. This needs to be the set of data that is the highest quality so that we can ensure that the algorithm is going to learn the right information along the way. Take your time to push the data through, maybe even doing it a few times so that the algorithm has more instances where it is able to learn how to behave in the process.

Testing the Data

After we have had some time to train our algorithm, and all of the training data has gone through that chosen algorithm, it is time to do some testing. Using a brand-new set of data (remember that we split our data up into two parts in the beginning), we will push the data through the algorithm to see what are the results we can get.

The accuracy level that we end up with here is going to tell us a lot of information. For example, it is going to let us know whether the algorithm was able to learn along the way, how well it learned, and how much more work we need to do to make this process accurate enough that we are able to rely on it along the way with the data analysis.

When you do the testing part of the process, you want to aim to get above 50 percent. You do not need to get all the way in the 90 or even the 100 percentile because this is going to happen with time, not with just one training and one testing session. Even if you get a number that is lower, like in the low 60 percent, then this is a good sign.

The assumption when you go through this is that any accuracy that is above 50 percent shows us that the algorithm was able to learn. We assume that even if the algorithm did not have any training at all, and we just jumped right in with the testing, the algorithm should be able to give us some results that are correct, at least half of the time. If you can get an accuracy that is above that, then this is a good sign that your training went well. You may need to go through it a few more times to get the accuracy up a bit more, but this is still a good sign.

If you do this, though, and your accuracy ends up below 50 percent, then we have a problem. The algorithm should never get below this much accuracy, and if you are getting these kinds of numbers, then it is likely that your training went wrong. These numbers usually indicate that your data is bad and that you did not get the high-quality data that you should have to start.

With these kinds of numbers, you need to go all the way back to the drawing board. Using the same kind of data to go through the process again is not going to do you or anyone else any good, and it can really cause some harm to the results that you get through this. It is probably best to go out and find some better data, data that is higher in quality. At the very least, you should take the time to rework your data and make sure that it is going to behave in the manner. Whether this means better organization, checking the missing values, cleaning it more, or picking out a different algorithm, there is something that needs to change when this starts to happen to you.

Hopefully, we do not have that last problem, and instead, we end up with an algorithm that learned something. It may not be as high of accuracy as we would like to start with, but it can be a good start. We will need to go through the process and get it higher, but if you can get any accuracy that is above 50 percent, then pat yourself on the back because you have started off on the right foot in this process.

Repeat the Process

Unfortunately, this is not where it all ends; getting 60 percent accuracy is not going to be an excuse to walk away and do nothing else with some of the work that you want to handle. It is a good start, but we need to rinse and repeat to get this higher. Our goal here is not to get it to 100 percent. That takes a long time and won't really happen until we put this into some of the real-world applications that we are hoping with these algorithms. However, if you are looking to use this as a way to make decisions and learn more about your industry, it is likely that you want the algorithm to start out with more accuracy than 60 percent.

So, how do we get the accuracy to be higher? We go through the same steps that we outlined above, many times over. When the first test is done, we go through and do another set of training, making sure that the data we rely on is strong and will provide us with the answers that we want. Then, when that training is all done, we go through and do another test, and hope that we are able to get a higher accuracy level in the process.

This is a process that we may have to repeat multiple times in order to get the accuracy that we want. The cool thing about machine learning, though, is that these algorithms are able to learn, and they will get better at some of the work they do; the more data that you feed to them, the more that they are able to learn from that information along the way. And as long as your training and testing data are higher in quality and are on the right topics, you will find that it is going to work in your favor, and the accuracy levels will go up.

The number of times that you need to go through this process will often depend on your own goals and what you are hoping to accomplish.

If you want to get the accuracy level up as high as possible before you start working with the algorithm, then you will need to do more iterations of the training and the testing.

If having a little bit lower accuracy is fine because you know the algorithm will have plenty of time to learn as it goes, then you may be able to get away with fewer iterations to get this done. It all depends on the type of project we are developing in the first place.

Working with the different algorithms that are present in data analysis is kind of fun and is one of the parts of the process that many people are excited to learn how to work with in the first place.

When you get to this part, we are finally going through the steps to learn how to make the algorithms behave so that you can use them to make smart business decisions for your needs.

While this part is exciting, it is important not to get ahead of yourself too much here.

You still need to take some precautions and think things through to ensure that you are doing it in the proper manner. If you rush through it, the accuracy is not going to be there, and you will not get the algorithms and more to behave in the manner that you would like.

However, this is going to be some of the fun stuff in the data analysis process, and you will quickly find as you work through these algorithms that this is exactly why we needed to take so much time to work on the data organization and cleaning that we talked about before.

It will ensure that this part of the process stays fun and that you can actually get some of the accurate results that are so important here.

The Fundamental Components of the Team Data Science Process

Definition of a Data Science Lifecycle

The five major stages of the TDSP lifecycle that outline the interactive steps required for project execution from start to finish are: "Business understanding," "Data acquisition in understanding," "modeling," "deployment," and "customer acceptance." Keep reading for details on this to come shortly!

Standardized Project Structure

To enable seamless and easy access to project documents for the team members allowing for quick retrieval of information, use of templates and a shared directory structure goes a long way; all the project documents and the project code our store and a "version control system" such as "TFS," "Git" or "Subversion" for improved team collaboration. Business requirements and associated tasks and functionalities are stored in an agile project tracking system like "JIRA," "Rally," and "Azure DevOps" to enable enhanced tracking of code for every single functionality. These tools also help in the estimation of resources and costs involved through the project lifecycle. To ensure effective management of each project, information security, and team collaboration, TDSP confers the creation of separate storage for each project on the version control system; the adoption of a standardized structure for all the projects within an organization aids in the creation of an institutional knowledge library across the organization.

The TDSP lifecycle provides standard templates for all the required documents as well as folder structure at a centralized location. The files containing programming codes for the data exploration and extraction of the functionality can be organized using the provided folder structure, which also holds records pertaining to model iterations. These templates allow the team members to easily understand the work that has been completed by others as well as for a seamless addition of new team members to a given project. The markdown format supports ease of accessibility as well as making edits or updates to the document templates. In order to make sure the project goal and objectives are well defined and also to ensure the expected quality of the deliverables, these templates provide various checklists with important questions for each project. For example, a "project charter" can be used to document the project scope and the business problem that is being resolved by the project; standardized data reports are used to document the "structure and statistics" of the data.

Infrastructure and Resources for Data Science Projects

To effectively store infrastructure and manage shared analytics, the TDSP recommends using tools like: "machine learning service," databases, "big data clusters," and cloud-based systems to store data sets. The analytics and storage infrastructure that houses raw as well as processed or cleaned data sets can be cloud-based or on-premises. D analytics and storage infrastructure permits the reproducibility of analysis and prevents duplication and the redundancy of data that can create inconsistency and unwarranted infrastructure costs. Tools are supplied to grant specific permissions to the shared resources and to track their activity, which in turn allows secure access to the resources for each member of the team.

Tools and Utilities for Project Execution

The introduction of any changes to an existing process tends to be rather challenging in most organizations. Several tools that are provided by the TDSP can be implemented to encourage and raise the consistency of the adoption of these changes. Some of the basic tasks in the data science lifecycle, including "data exploration" and "baseline modeling" can be easily automated with the tools provided by TDSP. To allow the hassle-free contribution of shared tools and utilities into the team's "shared code repository," TDSP provides a well-defined structure. This results in cost savings by allowing other project teams within the organization to reuse and repurpose these shared tools and utilities.

The TDSP lifecycle serves as a standardized template with a well-defined set of artifacts that can be used to garner effective team collaboration and communication across the board. This lifecycle is comprised of a selection of the best practices and structures from "Microsoft" to facilitate the successful delivery of predictive analytics solutions and intelligent applications. Let's look at the details of each of the five stages of the TDSP lifecycle, namely, "Business understanding," "Data acquisition in understanding," "modeling," "deployment," and "customer acceptance."

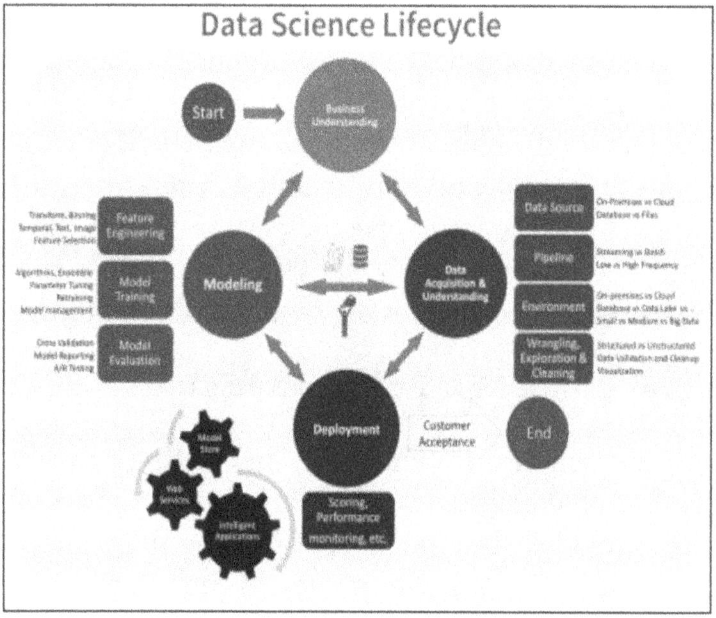

Business Understanding

The goal of this stage is to gather and drill down on the essential variables that will be used as targets for the model, and the metrics associated with these variables will ultimately determine the overall success of the project. Another significant objective of this stage is the identification of required data sources that the company already has or may need to procure. At this stage, the two primary tasks that are required to be accomplished are: "defining objects and identifying data sources."

Defining Objectives

All projects must always start with the identification of the key business variables that the analytical tools are required to predict. These variables are called "model targets," and the metrics associated with these model targets, such as sales forecast and prediction of fraudulent orders, are used as a measure of the success of the project. It is imperative to define the project goals and objectives, to work with the stakeholders and the end-users, and to ask relevant questions that can be highly specific or even vague. The data science approach employs names and numbers to answer these questions. The five types of questions that are primarily used for data science or machine learning are pertaining to: "regression (how much or how many?), classification (what categories?), clustering (which groups?), anomaly detection (is this unusual?), recommendation (which option should be taken?)". It is important to determine the right questions for your project and understand how the answers to these questions will help you accomplish the business or project goals. Specification and alignment of the roles and responsibilities of each member within the project team are quintessential to the success of the project. This can be accomplished with the help of a high-level project plan containing significant milestones that can be modified as needed for the course of the project. Another important definition that should be agreed upon at this stage of the project is that of all key performance indicators and metrics. For example, a project for prediction of customer turnover rate requiring the accuracy rate of "ABC" percent by the completion of the project can help you understand the requirement that must be fulfilled to meet the success criteria of the project. So in order to achieve the "ABC" percent accuracy rate, the company may run discount offers and promotions.

The industry-wide standard used in the development of metrics is called "SMART," which stands for "Specific, Measurable, Achievable, Relevant, Time-bound."

Identification of Data Sources

The data sources that may contain "known examples" of answers to the five types of questions raised during the defining phase must be identified and accounted for. You must look for data that is in direct relevance to the questions asked and assess if you have a measurable target and features related to those targets.

The data that serves as an accurate measure for the model target and its features is crucial for the determination of the project's success. For example, you might encounter a situation where the existing system is unable to collect and record the types of data that are required to accomplish the project goals. This should immediately inform you that you need to start looking for external data sources or run a system update to enable the collection of additional data types by the existing system.

Deliverables to Be Created in This Stage

Charter Document

It is a "living document" that needs to be updated throughout the course of the project, in light of new project discoveries and changing business requirements. A standard template is supplied with the TDSP "project structure definition." It is important to build upon this document by adding more details throughout the course of the project while keeping the stakeholders updated promptly on all changes made.

Data Sources

Within the TDSP "project data report folder," the data sources can be found within the "Raw Data Sources" section of the "Data Definitions Report." The "Raw Data Sources" section also specifies the initial and final locations of the raw data and provide additional details like the "coding scripts" to move up the data to any desired environment.

Data Dictionaries

The descriptions of the characteristics and features of the data such as the "data schematics" and available "entity-relationship diagrams," provided by the stakeholders are documented within the Data dictionaries.

Data Acquisition and Understanding

The goal of this stage is the production of high-quality processed data set with defined relationships to the model targets and location of the data set in the required analytics environment. At this stage, the "solution architecture" of the data pipeline must also be developed, which will allow regular updates to and scoring of the data. The three primary tasks that must be completed during this stage are: "Data ingestion, Data exploration, and Data pipeline set up."

Data ingestion

The process required to transfer the data from the source location to the target location should be set up in this phase. The target locations are determined by the environments that will allow you to perform analytical activities like training and predictions.

Data exploration

The data set must be scrubbed to remove any discrepancies and errors before it can be used to train the Data models. To check the data quality and gathered information required to process the data before modeling, tools such as data summarization and visualization should be used. Since this process is repeated multiple times, an automated utility called "IDEAR," which is provided by TDSP can be used for Data visualization and creation of Data summary reports. With the achievement of satisfactory quality of the processed data, the inherent data patterns can be observed. This, in turn, helps in the selection and development of an appropriate "predictive model" for the target.

Now you must assess if you have the required amount of data to start the modeling process, which is iterative in nature and may require you to identify new data sources to achieve higher relevance and accuracy.

Set up a Data Pipeline

To supplement the iterative process of data modeling, a standard process for scoring new data and refreshing the existing data set must be established by setting up a "data pipeline or workflow."

The solution architecture of the data pipeline must be developed by the end of this stage. There are three types of pipelines that can be used on the basis of the business needs and constraints of the existing system: "batch-based," "real-time or streaming," and "hybrid."

Deliverables to Be Created in This Stage

Data Quality Report

This report must include a "data summary" relationship between the business requirement and its attributes and variable ranking, among other details. The "IDEAR" tool supplied with TDSP it's capable of generating data quality reports on a relational table, CSV file, or any other tabular data set.

Solution Architecture

A description or a diagram of the data pipeline that is used to score new data and generated predictions after the model has been built can be referred to as "solution architecture." This diagram can also provide the data pipeline needed to "retrain" the model based on new data.

Checkpoint Decision

Prior to that start of the actual model building process project must be reevaluated to determine if the expected value can be achieved by pursuing the project. These are also called "Go or No-Go" decisions.

Modeling

The goal of this stage is to find "optimal data features" for the machine learning model, which is informative enough to predict the target variables accurately and can be deployed in the production environment. The three primary tasks that must be accomplished in this stage are: "feature engineering, model training, and the determination of the suitability of the model for the production environment."

Feature Engineering

The data features must be created from the raw data variables using the process of “inclusion, aggregation, and transformation.” To be able to understand the functioning of the model, a clear understanding of how these data features relate to one another as well as to the machine learning algorithms that will be using those features must be developed. The insights gathered from the data exploration phase can be combined with the domain expertise to allow creative feature engineering.

The fine art of determining and including informative variables while making sure a whole lot of unrelated variables are not included in the data set is referred to as feature engineering.

Too many unrelated variables will add noise to the data model, so an attempt must be made to add as many informative variables as possible to get better results. The features must also be generated for any new data collected doing the scoring.

Model Training

A wide variety of modeling algorithms are available in the market today. The algorithm that meets the criteria of your project must be selected. The process for “model training” can be divided into four steps which are:

- Create a “training data set” as well as a “test data set” by appropriately dividing the input data.
- Development of the model with the use of the “training data set.”

- Evaluation of the training and the test data set by employing various machine learning algorithms as well as related "tuning parameters" that are designed to help answer the previously discussed five types of questions from the existing data set.

- Assess the best fit for the solution to resolve the business problem by comparing all available methods using key performance indicators and metrics.

TDSP provides an "automated modeling and reporting tool" that is capable of running through multiple algorithms and "parameters sweeps" to develop a "baseline model" as well as a "baseline modeling report" that can serve as a performance summary for each "model and parameter combination."

Deliverables to Be Created in This Stage

Feature Sets

The document containing all the features described in the "feature sets section of the data definition report."

It is heavily used by the programmers to write the required code and develop features based on the basis of the description provided by the document.

Model Report

This document must contain the details of each model that was evaluated based on a standard template report.

Checkpoint Decisions

A decision regarding the deployment of the model to the production environment must be made on the basis of the performance of different models.

Deployment

The goal of this stage is to release the solution models to lower production-like environments such as the pre-production environment and user acceptance testing environment before eventually deploying the model in the production environment. The primary task to be accomplished in this stage is the "operationalization of the model."

Operationalize the Model

Once you have obtained a set of models with expected performance levels, these models can then be operationalized for other applicable applications to use.

According to the business requirements, predictions can be made in real-time or on a batch basis. In order to deploy the model, they must be integrated with an open "Application Programming Interface" (API) to allow interaction of the model with all other applications and its components, as needed.

Deliverables to Be Created in This Stage

It is necessary to create the following:

- A dashboard report; using the key performance indicators and metrics to access the health of the system.

- A document or run book, this will contain the details of the deployment plan for the final model.
- Create a document containing the solution architecture of the final model.

Customer Acceptance

The goal of this stage is to ensure that the final solution for the project meets the expectations of the stakeholders and fulfills the business requirements gathered during Stage I of the Data science lifecycle. The two primary tasks that must be accomplished in this stage are: "system validation and project hand-off."

System Validation

The final solution that will be deployed in the production environment must be evaluated against the business requirements and the data pipeline to make sure that the stakeholders needs are met. The stakeholder must validate that the system meets their business needs and resolves the problem that started the project in the first place. All the documentation must be thoroughly reviewed and finalized by the end of this stage.

Project Hand-off

At this stage, the project must be transferred from the development team to the post-production and maintenance team.

For example, IT support team or someone from the stakeholder's team DAD will provide day-to-day support for the solution in the production environment.

Deliverables to Be Created in This Stage

The most important document created during this stage is for the stakeholders and called an "exit report." The document contains all of the available details of the project that are significant to provide an understanding of the operations of the system. TDSP supplies a standardized template for the "exit report" that can be easily customized to cater to specific stakeholder needs.

Types of Data

Now that you understand the importance of data science let us look at different types of data so you can choose the most appropriate analytical tools and algorithms for the type of data that needs to be processed. Data types can be divided into two at a very high level: qualitative and quantitative.

Qualitative Data

Any data that cannot be measured and only observed subjectively by adding a qualitative feature to the object it's called "qualitative data." It is the classification of an object using unmeasurable features results in the creation of qualitative data.

For example, attributes like color, smell, texture, and taste. There are three types of qualitative data:

Binary or Binomial Data

Data values that signal mutually exclusive events where only one of the two categories or options is correct and applicable. For example, true or false, yes or no, positive or negative. Consider a box of assorted tea bags.

You try all the different flavors and group the ones that you like as "good" and the ones you don't as "bad." In this case, "good or bad" would be categorized as the "binomial data" type. This type of data is widely used in the development of statistical models for predictive analysis.

Nominal or Unordered Data

Data characteristics that lack an "implicit or natural value" can be referred to as nominal data. Consider a box of M&Ms, you can record the color of each M&M in the box in a worksheet, and that would serve as nominal data.

This kind of data is widely used to assess statistical differences in the data set, using techniques like "Chi-Square analysis," which could tell you "statistically significant differences" in the amount of each color of M&M in a box.

Ordered or Ordinal Data

The characteristics of this Data type do have certain "implicit or natural of value" such as small, medium, or large. For example, online reviews on the sites like "Yelp," "Amazon," and "Trip Advisor" have a rating scale from 1 to 5, implying a 5-star rating is better than 4, which is better than 3, and so on.

Quantitative Data

Any characteristics of the data that can be measured objectively are called "quantitative data." It is the classification of an object in using measurable features and giving it a numerical value results and creation of quantitative data.

For example, product prices, temperature, dimensions like length, etc.

There are two types of quantitative data:

Continuous Data

Data values that can be defined to a further lower level, such as units of measurement like kilometers, meters, centimeters, and on and on, are called continuous data type. For example, you can purchase a bag of almonds by weight like 500 g or 8 ounces. This accounts for continuous data type, which is primarily used to test and verify different kinds of hypotheses such as assessing the accuracy of the weight printed on the bag of almonds.

Discrete Data

The numerical data value that cannot be divided and reduced to a higher level of precision, such as the number of cars owned by a person which can only be accounted for as indivisible numbers (you cannot have 1.5 or 2.3 cars), is called as discrete data types. For example, you can purchase another bag of ice cream bars by the number of ice cream bars inside the package, like four or six.

This accounts for the discrete data type, which can be used in combination with the continuous data type to perform a regression analysis to verify if the total weight of the ice cream box (continuous data) is correlated with the number of ice cream bars (discrete data) inside.

Data Science Strategies

Data science is mainly used in decision-making by making precise predictions with the use of “predictive causal analytics,” “prescriptive analytics,” and machine learning.

Predictive Causal Analytics

The “predictive causal analytics” can be applied to develop a model that can accurately predict and forecast the likelihood of a particular event occurring in the future.

For example, financial institutions use predictive causal analytics-based tools to assess the likelihood of a customer defaulting on their credit card payments by generating a model that can analyze the payment history of the customer with all of their borrowing institutions.

Prescriptive Analytics

The “prescriptive analytics” is widely used in the development of “intelligent tools and applications” that are capable of modifying and learning with dynamic parameters and make their own “decisions.” The tool not only predicts the occurrence of a future event but is also capable of providing recommendations on a variety of actions and its resulting outcomes. For example, the self-driving cars gather driving-related data with every driving experience and use it to train themselves to make better driving and maneuvering decisions.

Machine Learning to Make Predictions

Machine learning algorithms are a necessity to develop models that can determine future trends based on the transactional data acquired by the company. This is considered as “supervised machine learning,” which we will elaborate on later in this book. For example, fraud detection systems use machine learning algorithms on the historical data pertaining to fraudulent purchases to detect if a transaction is fraudulent.

Machine Learning for Pattern Discovery

To be able to develop models that are capable of identifying hidden data patterns but lack required parameters to make future predictions, the "unsupervised machine learning algorithms," such as "Clustering," need to be employed.

For example, telecom companies often use the "clustering" technology to expand their network by identifying network tower locations with optimal signal strength in the targeted region.

Data Science Versus Data Analysis

The terms data science and data analytics are often used interchangeably. However, these terms are completely different and have different implications for different businesses. Data science encompasses a variety of scientific models and methods that can be used to manipulate and analyze structured, semi-structured, and unstructured data. Tools and processes that can be used to make sense of gather insight from highly complex, unorganized, and raw data set fall under the umbrella of data science. Unlike data analytics that is targeted to verify a hypothesis, data science boils down to connecting data points to identify new patterns and insights that can be made use of in future planning for the business. Data science moves the business from inquiry to insights by providing a new perspective into their structured and unstructured data by identifying patterns that can allow businesses to increase efficiencies, reduce costs and recognize the new market opportunities.

Data science acts as a multidisciplinary blend of technology, machine learning algorithm development, statistical analysis, and data inference that provides businesses with enhanced capability to solve their most complex business problems. Data analytics falls under the umbrella of data science and pertains more to reviewing and analyzing historical data to put it in context. Unlike data science, data analytics is characterized by low usage of artificial intelligence, predictive modeling, and machine learning algorithms to gather insights from processed and structured data using standard SQL query commands. The seemingly nuanced differences between data analytics and data science can actually have a substantial impact on an organization.

Data Science in Cyber Security

The ability to analyze and closely examine Data trends and patterns using Machine learning algorithms has resulted in the significant application of data science in the cybersecurity space. With the use of data science, companies are not only able to identify the specific network terminal(s) that initiated the cyber-attack but are also in a position to predict potential future attacks on their systems and take required measures to prevent the attacks from happening in the first place. Use of "active intrusion detection systems" that are capable of monitoring users and devices on any network of choice and flag any unusual activity serves as a powerful weapon against hackers and cyber attackers. At the same time, the "predictive intrusion detection systems" that are capable of using machine learning algorithms on historical data to detect potential security threats serves as a powerful shield against cyber predators.

Cyber-attacks can result in a loss of priceless data and information resulting in extreme damage to the organization. Sophisticated encryption and complex signatures can be used to secure and protect the data set and prevent unauthorized access. Data science can help with the development of such impenetrable protocols and algorithms. By analyzing the trends and patterns of previous cyber-attacks on companies across different industrial sectors, Data science can help detect the most frequently targeted data set and even predict potential future cyber-attacks. Companies rely heavily on the data generated and authorized by their customers, but in the light of increasing cyber-attacks, customers are extremely wary of their personal information being compromised and are looking to take their businesses to the companies that are able to assure them of their data security and privacy by implementing advanced data security tools and technologies. This is where data science is becoming the saving grace of the companies by helping them enhance their cybersecurity measures.

A Practical Example of Working with Python Data Science

Now that we have spent some time taking a look at data science and the Python language, it is time to work with an example of how we can bring this all together and work on our own project with data science.

In this one, we are going to work to anticipate the circumstance of diabetes in patients and then take the right measures ahead of time to help prevent this issue. In this use case, we are going to spend our time figuring out the occurrence of diabetes with the help of an entire lifecycle that we talked about earlier in this guidebook. Some of the steps that we need to work with will be below:

First, we need to make sure that we can compile the data found on the medical history that comes with the patient. This is going to be the research that will create and test out our model and can help us later if we need to submit some information on a new patient. We are going to use the sample data that is available below to help us create this kind of model:

```
;npreg;glu;bp;skin;bmi;ped;age,income
1;6;148;72;35;33.6;0.627;50
2;1;85;66;29;26.6;0.351;31
3;1;89;80;23;28.1;0.167;21
4;3;78;50;32;31;0.248;26
5;2;197;70;45;30.5;0.158;53
6;5;166;72;19;25.8;0.587;51
7;0;118;84;47;45.8;0.551;31
8;1;103;30;38;43.3;0.183;33
9;3;126;88;41;39.3;0.704;27
10;9;119;80;35;29;0.263;29
11;1;97;66;15;23.2;0.487;22
12;5;109;75;26;36;0.546;60
13;3;88;58;11;24.8;0.267;22
14;10;122;78;31;27.6;0.512;45
15;4;97;60;33;24;0.966;33
16;9;102;76;37;32.9;0.665;46
17;2;90;68;42;38.2;0.503;27
18;4;111;72;47;37.1;1.39;56
19;3;180;64;25;34;0.271;26
20;7;106;92;18;39;0.235;48
21;9;171;110;24;45.4;0.721;54
```

There are going to be a lot of attributes that we need to work on within the data set above. These can include:

Npreg

This is the number of times the patient has been pregnant.

Glucose

This is going to include the plasma glucose concentration.

Bp

This is the blood pressure of the patient.

Skin

This is going to be the tricep skinfold thickness.

Bmi

This is going to include the body mass index of the patient.

Ped

This is going to be the diabetes pedigree function of the patient.

Age

This is going to include the age of the patient.

Income

This takes a look at the income of the patient.

What the Cloud Is

Cloud can be described as a global server network, each having different unique functions. Understanding networks is required to study the cloud. Networks can be simple or complex clusters of information or data.

As specified earlier, networks can have a simple or small group of computers connected or large groups of computers connected. The largest network can be the Internet. The small groups can be home local networks like Wi-Fi and Local Area Network that are limited to certain computers or locality. There are shared networks such as media, web pages, app servers, data storage, and printers, and scanners. Networks have nodes, where a computer is referred to as a node. The communication between these computers is established by using protocols. Protocols are the intermediary rules set for a computer. Protocols like HTTP, TCP, and IP are used on a large scale. All the information is stored on the computer, but it becomes difficult to search for information on the computer every time. Such information is usually stored in a data Centre. Data Centre is designed in such a way that it is equipped with support security and protection for the data. Since the cost of computers and storage has decreased substantially, multiple organizations opt to make use of multiple computers that work together that one wants to scale. This differs from other scaling solutions like buying other computing devices. The intent behind this is to keep the work going continuously even if a computer fails; the other will continue the operation. There is a need to scale some cloud applications, as well, having a broad look at some computing applications like YouTube, Netflix, and Facebook that require some scaling. We rarely experience such applications failing, as they have set up their systems on the cloud. There is a network cluster in the cloud, where many computers are connected to the same networks and accomplish similar tasks. You can call it a single source of information or a single computer that manages everything to improve performance, scalability, and availability.

Data Science in the Cloud

The whole process of Data Science takes place in the local machine, i.e., a computer or laptop provided to the data scientist. The computer or laptop has inbuilt programming languages and a few more prerequisites installed. This can include common programming languages and some algorithms.

The data scientist later has to install relevant software and development packages as per his/her project. Development packages can be installed using managers such as Anaconda or similar managers. You can opt for installing them manually too.

Once you install and enter into the development environment, then your first step, i.e., the workflow, starts where your companion is only data. It is not mandatory to carry out the task related to Data Science or Big data on different development machines. Check out the reasons behind this:

- The processing time required to carry out tasks in the development environment fails due to processing power failure.

- Get the presence of large data sets that cannot be contained in the development environment's system memory.

- Deliverables must be arrayed into a production environment and incorporated as a component in a large application.

- It is advised to use a machine that is fast and powerful.

Data scientist explores many options when they face such issues; they make use of on-premise machines or virtual machines that run on the cloud. Using virtual machines and auto-scaling clusters has various benefits, such as they can span up and discard it anytime in case it is required. Virtual machines are customized in a way that will fulfill one's computing power and storage needs. Deployment of the information in a production environment to push it in a large data pipeline may have certain challenges. These challenges are to be understood and analyzed by the data scientist. This can be understood by having a gist of software architectures and quality attributes.

Software Architecture and Quality Attributes

A cloud-based software system is developed by Software Architects. Such systems may be product or service that depends on the computing system. If you are building software, the main task includes the selection of the right programming language that is to be programmed. The purpose of the system can be questioned; hence, it needs to be considered. Developing and working with software architecture must be done by a highly skilled person. Most organizations have started implementing effective and reliable cloud environment using cloud computing. These cloud environments are deployed over to various servers, storage, and networking resources. This is used in abundance due to its less cost and high ROI. The main benefit to data scientists or their teams is that they are using the big space in the cloud to explore more data and create important use cases. You can release a feature and have it tested the next second and check whether it adds value or it is not useful to carry forward. All this immediate action is possible due to cloud computing.

Sharing Big Data in the Cloud

The role of Big Data is also vital while dealing with the cloud as it makes it easier to track and analyze insights. Once this is established, big data creates great value for users.

The traditional way was to process wired data. It became difficult for the team to share their information with this technique. The usual problems included transferring large amounts of data and collaboration of the same. This is where cloud computing started sowing its seed in the competitive world. All these problems were eliminated due to cloud computing, and gradually, teams were able to work together from different locations and overseas as well. Therefore, cloud computing is very vital in both Data Science as well as Big data. Most organizations make use of the cloud. To illustrate, a few companies that use the cloud are Swiggy, Uber, Airbnb, *etc.* They use cloud computing for sharing information and data.

Cloud and Big Data Governance

Working with the cloud is a great experience as it reduces resource cost, time, and manual efforts. But the question arises that how organizations deal with security, compliance, governance? Regulation of the same is a challenge for most companies.

Not limited to Big data problems, but working with the cloud also has its issues related to privacy and security. Hence, it is required to develop a strong governance policy in your cloud solutions. To ensure that your cloud solutions are reliable, robust, and governable, you must keep it as an open architecture.

Need for Data Cloud Tools to Deliver High Value of Data

The demand for data scientists in this era is increasing rapidly. They are responsible for helping big and small organizations to develop useful information from the data or data set that is provided. Large organizations carry massive data that must be analyzed continuously. As per recent reports, almost 80% of the unstructured data received by the organizations is in the form of social media, emails, i.e., Outlook, Gmail, etc., videos, images, *etc*. With the rapid growth of cloud computing, data scientists deal with various new workloads that come from IoT, AI, Blockchain, Analytics, *etc*. Pipeline. Working with all these new workloads requires a stable, efficient, and centralized platform across all teams. With all this, there is a need for managing and recording new data as well as legacy documents. Once a data scientist is given a task, and he/she has the dataset to work on, he/she must possess the right skills to analyze the ever-increasing volumes through cloud technologies. They need to convert the data into useful insights that would be responsible for uplifting the business. The data scientist has to build an algorithm and code the program. They mostly utilize 80% of their time to gathering information, creating and modifying data, cleaning if required, and organizing data. Rest 20% is utilized for analyzing the data with effective programming. This calls for the requirement of having specific cloud tools to help the data scientist to reduce their time searching for appropriate information. Organizations should make available new cloud services and cloud tools to their respective data scientists so that they can organize massive data quickly. Therefore, cloud tools are very important for a data scientist to analyze large amounts of data in a shorter period. It will save the company's time and help build strong and robust data Models.

Training Testing and Repeating

Now that we have had a chance to spend time looking for the data that we want to use and that we have had a chance to clean and organize all of our data, it is time to move on to the part that is a bit more fun in the process. It is time for us to look a bit more at the fun part. We are going to look at some of the fun things that we are able to do when it comes to our algorithms and making sure that they are able to provide us with some of the accurate results that we are able to handle with this.

There is actually a good deal of work that we need to do when it comes to working with our algorithms. You can't just push the data through and assume it is going to provide us with a few of the different options that we want along with the way. These algorithms are not going to be set up to provide us with accurate results right off the bat. We need to be able to go through and really look through, doing the training and the testing of the algorithms to help us increase the accuracy. When the accuracy is high enough, only then are we able to go through and really see some amazing results with our algorithms.

With this in mind, let's take a closer look at some of the steps that we need to take in order to get this done and to ensure that we are able to really get these algorithms to work well in the long run.

Chapter 5.

Alternative Data

Data Exploration

When you start analyzing a dataset, you need to perform an exploratory data analysis in order to understand it the best you can.

This involves paying attention to its features, shape, confirm your hypothesis, and build your focus towards the next steps.

For the sake of consistency, for this phase, we are going to reuse the iris dataset we created in an earlier section. So let's start by importing it:

```
In: import pandas as pd

iris_filename = 'datasets-uci-iris.csv'

iris = pd.read_csv(iris_filename, header=None,

names= ['sepal_length', 'sepal_width',

'petal_length', 'petal_width', 'target'])

iris.head()
```

Out:

Now let's start exploring! We're going to start by using the "describe" method as following:

In: iris.describe()

You will now see a number of numerical features, like the number of observations, average value, deviation, min/max values, and more. Let's get a better look at this data by looking at a graph representation of what we have. You can do this with the help of the "boxplot" method.

In: boxes = iris.boxplot(return_type='axes')

This step isn't in any way necessary, but visualization of data can be extremely helpful. Next, we can take a look at the connection between the features by using a similarity matrix. You can do this with the following command:

In: pd.crosstab(iris['petal_length'] > 3.758667, iris['petal_width'] > 1.198667)

In this example, we are counting how many times the "petal_length" appears more than the average of the same count for the "petal_width."

This is done with the "crosstab" method, and the result should display that there's a strong relationship between the two features. If you want to, you can see the result graphically as well by using the following code lines:

In: scatterplot = iris.plot(kind='scatter', x='petal_width',

y='petal_length', s=64, c='blue', edgecolors='white')

Out:

This will show you that the x and y are in a strong relationship. You make the same conclusion when you look at the data; however, as previously said, visualization is much more helpful.

Next, let's check the distribution by using a histogram. Type the following code:

In: distr = iris.petal_width.plot(kind='hist', alpha=0.5, bins=20)

Why did we choose 20 bins, and what are they? In histograms, bins are simply the intervals of a variable. The general idea is to calculate the square root of the number of observations, and that will be your number of bins.

Creating New Features

You won't always encounter situations where there's a close relationship between the features, like in the example above. This is why you need to learn how to apply transformations that will lead to an accuracy improvement. As usual, let's go through an example to illustrate this concept. Imagine you're working out how much a certain house is worth on the market. You have all the dimensions of every room, and from this data, you want to create a feature that stands for the total volume of the house. The difference between the dimension features such as height and width and volume feature is that the dimensions are observable, but volume isn't. However, you can determine the volume of the house based on the existing features.

In: import numpy as np

```
from sklearn import datasets

from sklearn.cross_validation import train_test_split

from sklearn.metrics import mean_squared_error

cali = datasets.california_housing.fetch_california_housing()

X = cali['data']

Y = cali['target']

X_train, X_test, Y_train, Y_test = train_test_split(X, Y, train_size=0.8)
```

In this example, we import a data set with house prices on the Californian real estate market. To solve this, we need to use a regressor and a mean absolute error of around 1.15. Don't worry if you don't fully understand the code for now. We will discuss regressors and mean absolute errors in the next chapter. For now, it's only important for you to understand the basis of the concept.

```
In: from sklearn.neighbors import KNeighborsRegressor

regressor = KNeighborsRegressor()

regressor.fit(X_train, Y_train)

Y_est = regressor.predict(X_test)

print ("MAE=", mean_squared_error(Y_test, Y_est))

Out: MAE= 1.15752795578
```

We have a mean absolute error of nearly 1.16 in the example. We want to try and lower that as much as possible. This can be achieved by using Z scores to normalize the features and make a regression comparison. This is referred to as Z normalization, and it involves the mapping of every feature to new features, but with a null mean and a unitary variance. Here's how this looks in code:

```
In: from sklearn.preprocessing import StandardScaler

scaler = StandardScaler()

X_train_scaled = scaler.fit_transform(X_train)

X_test_scaled = scaler.transform(X_test)

regressor = KNeighborsRegressor()

regressor.fit(X_train_scaled, Y_train)

Y_est = regressor.predict(X_test_scaled)

print ("MAE=", mean_squared_error(Y_test, Y_est))

Out: MAE= 0.432334179429
```

As you can see, we significantly reduced the error to under 0.5.

There are other ways to do this and to reduce the error down even more.

The process would involve more complex transformations, and there's no point advancing in that direction right now because it's not the purpose of this section.

All you need to understand is that applying transformation is crucial for an exploratory data analysis.

Dimensionality Reduction

What happens when you have a dataset with too many features that aren't really necessary?

Sometimes features don't contain information that is relevant, and they are basically noise. Reducing this noise is vital because it will make your dataset easier to manage, and your data will come out with more accuracy and with less noise. Dimensionality reduction is just right for this purpose. It is used to eliminate features and therefore improve the time it takes to perform the process.

Covariance Matrix

When you have several groups of features, you will need to search for the correlation between them. This is what the covariance matrix is used for. As already mentioned, one of the purposes of dimensionality reduction is to learn which features have a strong relationship with each other. By doing so, you will automatically know which features are of little to no use, and you can remove them.

We will stick to our previous "iris" dataset, where we have four features for every observation.

We'll be able to use a correlation matrix in such an example and see the results through a visual graph. Here's what the code looks like:

```
In: from sklearn import datasets

import numpy as np

iris = datasets.load_iris()
```

```
cov_data = np.corrcoef(iris.data.T)

print (iris.feature_names)

print (cov_data)
```

Out:

```
['sepal length (cm)', 'sepal width (cm)', 'petal length (cm)',

'petal width (cm)']

[[ 1. -0.10936925 0.87175416 0.81795363]

[-0.10936925 1. -0.4205161 -0.35654409]

[ 0.87175416 -0.4205161 1. 0.9627571 ]

[ 0.81795363 -0.35654409 0.9627571 1. ]]
```

Now that we have our covariance matrix let's use some more code to turn it into a graphical representation.

```
In: import matplotlib.pyplot as plt

img = plt.matshow(cov_data, cmap=plt.cm.rainbow)

plt.colorbar(img, ticks=[-1, 0, 1], fraction=0.045)

for x in range(cov_data.shape[0]):

for y in range(cov_data.shape[1]):

plt.text(x, y, "%0.2f" % cov_data[x,y],

size=12, color='black', ha="center", va="center")

plt.show()
```

Out:

The result of this code is a heat map, and inside it, we can see that the primary diagonal value is 1. Why? Because we normalized each feature covariance to 1. You will notice that there's a strong correlation between some of the features, namely feature one and feature three, feature one and feature four, and lastly feature three and feature four. Take notice that we also have feature two that appears to be independent of the rest who are in some kind of relationship with each other. This information can be used to compress the duplicated data and shrink the number down to only two features.

Gathering Your Data

The first thing that we need to take a look at is how to gather up the data that we need to accomplish this kind of process in data science. We need to have a chance to go through and look at our data, figure out what kind of data is out there that we can use, and so much more. But figuring out where to get that data, how much to collect, and what kind is going to be right to help us figure out more about our customers and industry can be hard.

There is an overabundance of options out there when it comes to the kind of data that we want to use along the way. We need to make sure that we are picking out the right kinds of data, rather than just collecting data because it is there and looks like the right thing to work with. When we are able to organize this in the manner that we need, and we make sure that we actually get the good data, even if it is not organized and structured the way that we want in the beginning, it is going to be so important.

That is why we are going to spend some time in this phase exploring what we are able to do with our data, how it is going to work for our needs and even some of the places where you can look in order to find the data that you would like to work with. With that in mind, we need to dive right in!

Know Your Biggest Business Problem

There is a lot of data out there, and it is not going to take long doing some searching before you find that you will end up in a rabbit hole with all of this information if you don't have a plan or a direction for what you are going to do with all of that information. There is a ton of good data, but if you just let it lead you rather than having a clear path in front of you, you are going to end up with a lot of problems and will never get the decision making help that you need.

If you have already gathered up your data, then this point is gone, and we just need to work from there. You can form through your biggest business problem, the one that you would like to spend your time focusing on and fixing, and then sort through the data there and see what changes you are able to make and what data out of that large source you have is going to make the biggest difference. Don't be scared to just leave some of the data for later, and don't let the fact that you may not use some of the data hold you back either.

During this time, we want to focus on knowing the best information; this is going to be the best way to make sure that you get the information needed to really propel your business into the future. Even some of the information is left behind, that is fine. You may come back to it later if you need some of it. But only the best data that you have should be used for your algorithms to give you the best results.

Now, if you have not had the time to go and collect any data yet, this is something we can work with as well. Forming the problem that you would like to solve and having a clear path can help you to sort through all of the noise that is out there and will ensure that you are really able to get things done in the process. You need to make sure that you are searching in the right places and looking for the information that is going to be the most critical for what you are trying to accomplish, the part that is going to be so important when it is time to handle some of the work that is out there.

Places to Look for the Data

The next thing that we need to consider when it comes to this process of gathering up the data and using it in the manner that we would like is figuring out where to find and look for the data that we need. There are actually so many different places where we are able to look for the data that we want to handle, but this is part of the beauty of the modern system that we are using today.

We have to remember, though, that most of the data that we will collect today is not going to be organized or structured. We will look at some of the steps that you are able to take in order to organize the data a little bit later, so this is not a big deal. Just be prepared that you will have to go through and take on a few extra steps in order to make sure that your data stays organized in the manner that you would like and that it is not going to be as nice and neat as you would like in the long run.

So, the places where you are able to look for some of the data that you would like to use in this process will be varied, and it often depends on what you are hoping to get out of this process. You want to concentrate on getting the highest-quality data in the process that you can, though. This is going to ensure that you are going to be able to find the data that you need and that the algorithms you use later on will really be able to provide you with some of the best results and insights that you need to move your business forward.

There are still a lot of places where you are able to look to find the data that you want. You will find that you can pick out data from websites (especially if you would like to work with web scraping), from social media sites if you are using one from surveys and focus groups of your own, and from other companies who may have collected the information and are using it to help out others along the way.

You may find that if you are able to bring up data from a more unique source as well, this is going to get you even further ahead with some of the work that you want to do. It will ensure that you will have data that no one else is going to have, and will provide you with some new patterns and insights, as long as you make sure that the data is high quality and will actually be good for your needs.

Store the Data

We also need to consider where we would like to store some of the data that we are working with along the way. You are likely to gather up a lot of data in the process, and it isn't likely that you just want to have it sitting around without a purpose or having it in a safe and secure location. This is especially true if you are working with data that is your own, data you got from surveys and other places that you don't want others getting ahold of.

There are a number of different places where you are able to store this data for your own needs, and the location that you choose is often going to depend on what works for you. If you have enough storage space on your own network, this can be a great place to start. Then the data is always safe and secure with you and easy to reach. You just need to make sure that you are keeping some good security measures on your system so you don't end up losing that information and no longer having it at your disposal.

Many companies decide to put it on a web-based storage area, like the cloud. This adds in another level of protection to the information and will ensure that you are able to reach that data when you need it as well. There are a lot of these kinds of storage areas that we can work with, and you will find that you are able to get this to work for some of your needs pretty well. Whether your storage needs are large or not, you will find that storing this data is going to make a world of difference when it is time to handle this process, and you just have to decide how much you would like to use ahead of time.

Knowing where to find the data that you need to start out with your data analysis and data science project is going to be super important. This is going to set the tone for the work that you are able to do later on and how much success you are going to have with your project as well. Make sure to search around for the data that is going to be needed in this, and pay attention to how much of it you will need, where you are likely to find it, and more.

Conclusion

Python programming language has rendered itself as the language of choice for coding beginners and advanced software programmers alike. This book is written to help you master the basic concepts of Python algorithms and how you can utilize your coding skills to analyze a large volume of data and uncover valuable information that can otherwise be easily lost in the volume.

When you have spent some time working on the Python language, and you are ready to take your skills to the next level and develop some strong codes that can do so much in just a few lines, make sure to read through this guidebook to help you get started!

Programming is a lot like language learning. You can be a very solid speaker of a language by acting minimally, sure. But it's only by devoting yourself to a language and immersing yourself in it that you'll be able to hang with the best in terms of your ability to speak that language.

This guidebook took some time to explore a lot of the different topics that can come up with this. It is meant to help us understand how to work with Python, what is all available with Python, and so much more. And with all of the great libraries and other extensions and features that come with this language, it is no wonder that there are so many things that you are able to do with the help of Python to make your own machine learning algorithms.

Python was designed primarily to emphasize the readability of the programming code, and its syntax enables programmers to convey ideas using fewer lines of code. Python programming language increases the speed of operation while allowing for higher efficiency in creating system integrations. The power of programming languages in our digital world cannot be underestimated. People are increasingly reliant on the modern conveniences of smart technology, and that momentum will endure for a long time. With all the instructions provided in this book, you are now ready to start developing your own innovative smart tech ideas and turn it into a major tech startup company and guide mankind towards a smarter future.

CPSIA information can be obtained
at www.ICGtesting.com
Printed in the USA
BVHW081206091220
595274BV00012B/1458

9 781801 326964